THUNDERBIRDS

THUNDERBIRDS

America's Living Legends of Giant Birds

Mark A. Hall

PARAVIEW PRESS

New York

Cover art by Mark Rollins
Cover design by smythtype
ISBN: 1-93104-497-X
Library of Congress Control Number: 2004112078

CONTENTS

Mark A. Hall on Thunderbirds

THE STUDY OF MYSTERIOUS, HIDDEN ANIMALS IS ONE of the newest life sciences, and certainly one of the most exciting. During the end of the last century and into the 21st century, interest in sightings and traditions dealing with "monsters" has moved from a shadowy world of travelogues to academic respectability. In the late 1940s, a young zoologist from Scotland, Ivan T. Sanderson, began using a word in his conversations with friends that gave a more formal sound to what had been called "romantic zoology" by natural history writers such as Willy Ley and Henry Wendt. Sanderson called this emerging discipline "cryptozoology."

In 1955, zoologist Bernard Heuvelmans, who is widely acknowledged as the "Father of Cryptozoology," wrote a groundbreaking book in his native French called *On the Track of Unknown Animals*. The book was soon reprinted in English and several other languages, and became an international bestseller. Concerned with eyewitness accounts, physical evidence, and aboriginal folklore on such animals as the Himalayan Yeti or Abominable Snowman, the Kenyan Spotted Lion or Marozi, and the Patagonian Giant Sloth, Heuvelmans made a good case for the fact that all of the world's animals had not yet been discovered. Despite the well-known success stories of the coelacanth, the okapi, and the giant panda, this really was a very novel idea at the time. Heuvelmans' concepts gained a wide audience, and followers of cryptozoology spread to all corners of the globe.

While Heuvelmans remained in Europe, cryptozoology's original leader, biologist Ivan T. Sanderson, established a small following from his home base in rural New Jersey. I began carrying on a detailed correspondence with Sanderson in 1961, as had others, and Sanderson would try to link his young correspondents, his "staff" of field investigators, with one another. This is how I came to be introduced to Mark A. Hall in the late 1960s. After I wrote Hall, we began corresponding regularly, and Hall traveled to Illinois to visit me, and then later I was able to visit him in Minnesota. We would spend hours, deep into the night, comparing notes from our field investigations, breaking reports from around the world, and archival materials—files and folders full of photographs, news articles, microfilmed items, and letters from witnesses and others. We would debate the evidence and theories, and share our thoughts on the state of emerging cryptozoology in those fresh new years of the science. Eventually Hall and I would coauthor one of the first studies of Native folklore on Sasquatch.

Hall was just a year older than me (Hall was born on Flag Day, June 14, 1946), and, like me, was passionate about archaeology, anthropology, zoology, and, of course, the discovery of new animals. Hall had been intrigued by nature's anomalies most of his life. Hall was also well traveled, having been in the intelligence services during the cold war (he doesn't like to talk about this much) and learned several languages, at one point translating Russian while serving in West Berlin. Back in the States and out of the service, Hall became an editor of the Minnesota Archaeological Society, and then an employee at the US Department of Agriculture, to give himself the financial security and time he needed to research and write about cryptozoology. Hall recently retired and moved to North Carolina, where he continues to edit his own journal, *Wonders*, and write about cryptozoology.

As a cryptozoological theorist, Mark A. Hall was the first to propose a new technique for studying cryptids (the unknown animals of cryptozoology) which he terms "telebiology." Of this method to study unknown primates, Hall wrote in his 1997 volume, *The Yeti, Bigfoot & True Giants*: "With temporary captives, we should do the best we can with them and then set them free. The results will be genuine knowledge in the records we will then have, *and* [emphasis is Hall's] we will have invested in the future of a new relationship with our primate relatives. This approach is part of what I have called 'telebiology,' a means by which we can begin to study the cryptids that have been the object of cryptozoology. If we make the effort to study animals at a distance, using our brains and technology, we can succeed where others have failed in the past. If we can accept that starting to study a species with a dead animal can be difficult, then we can put that goal at the end of the process instead of making it a requirement to do anything at all."

In *Thunderbirds*, Mark A. Hall reviews, for the first time, in one place, all that we know about the reality of large, condor-like birds, which have been reported for centuries in the Americas. For decades, Hall has researched the subject of these large birds and their allies (the giant owls). His tour of the accounts is masterful, for he places them in a context others never have.

Thunderbirds are few and far between today. We know that when California condors were more numerous, they apparently moved around more than they do now. In *Extinct and Vanishing Birds of the World* (1958), James C. Greenway Jr. observes: "In the past, a hundred and more years ago, there may have been a seasonal movement of population. This would account for the appearance of the birds near the Columbia River in Oregon in certain seasons." Greenway cites records of "great congregations of birds in the autumn, particularly where food was plentiful." Mark A. Hall paints a similar picture for the large unknown birds he profiles in his book. They were more numerous in the past, and what we see today is a mere shadow of their former numbers. But they were there, and Hall's case that there are a few left is a well-constructed and supported one.

Hall also shines a light on the most likely candidate for Thunderbirds, the prehistoric giants, the recently extinct teratorns. The long list of Thunderbird and other big bird sightings collected over the years may have to be reexamined someday by ornithologists. But for now, Hall's work preserves the record of the flight of the Thunderbirds.

Loren Coleman
Portland, Maine
March 28, 2004

CHAPTER 1

They Came from the Sky

SOME VERY LARGE BIRDS ARE BEING SIGHTED IN THE skies over North America.

For example, in October 2002 a spectacular bird was reported over southwestern Alaska with a wingspan that was estimated to be 14 feet (4.2 meters). It was seen more than once by villagers in Togiak and Manokotak. The bird created a news sensation until the authorities threw cold water on the reports. Since they didn't recognize any such bird, they said it could only have been a Steller's sea eagle, a bird no larger than 8 feet (2.4 meters) across its wings.

The first eyewitness to go on record was Moses Coupchiak on October 10. Coupchiak saw the bird flying toward him from a distance. His impression was that it was a plane, but then it banked left and he saw that it was a huge bird. His first impulse was to get on his radio and warn people in Togiak that their children should stay away from the area.

It was reported again the following week. John Bouker, the owner of Bristol Bay Air Service, was flying a plane into Manokotak when he and his passengers all saw a large bird. Bouker had been skeptical of the earlier reports but the sight of it changed his mind. He said, "He's really, really big. You wouldn't want your children out." The bird's wingspan was about the length of one of the wings on his Cessna 207, making it 14 feet (4.2 meters) across. One of his passengers was Nicolai Alakayak, who compared the bird's appearance to an eagle, but the size of "a little Super Cub." [1]

Alaska is a vast land of forests and mountains where the appearance of a mystery bird might be possible, but there are other reports that describe large birds in the 48 contiguous states. One of them was taken down in 2001 by Allison Jornlin. The sighting took place in Wisconsin in 1988. The witness waited 13 years to tell it, something that isn't unusual for observers of such peculiar wildlife. The witness, Kevin W., told Jornlin that he was 25 when he saw a giant bird while looking through a window in Elmbrook Memorial Hospital in Brookfield. Jornlin gave his description of the bird: "The enormous creature continued sailing closer. It did not flap its wings, but glided on air currents, always just underneath the clouds, as if 'using them for cover.' Kevin estimates the creature's wingspan was 12 to 15 feet [3.6 to 4.6 meters] across, with a similar span from its head to the tip of its tail." [2]

Giant birds have also turned up in Pennsylvania. In Wyoming County in late June 2002, two huge birds were seen to land at the top of a tree, bending a limb with their weight. Their wingspans were estimated to be 12 feet (3.6 meters). [3]

When the "super-eagle" was reported in Alaska, a federal biologist, Karen Laing, was quoted as observing that people "don't always have the sizes right, but this is very different because the people in that area know what eagles look like. I don't know of any bird that's three times the size of an eagle. What would that be? What bird occurs here that would possibly be three times the size of an eagle or the size of a Super Cub?"

The answer is the legendary Thunderbird, a giant bird known throughout history to the Eskimos and American Indians in North America. American pioneers encountered it in past centuries, and reports of them have continued to this day, begging us to ask: What is this bird and why is it reported in so many places? These and other questions will be answered here as we consider the history of giant birds of prey and the menace such huge birds could pose for human beings.

Popular fiction and movies can conjure up frightening images in the mind's eye and on the silver screen. An image not easily forgotten is that of a human being helpless in the clutches of some flying monster. This thought may make you shiver, but you nevertheless relax when you put down the book or turn away from the movie. But should you? Have human beings ever lived in fear

The modern Thunderbird as described in sightings during the past two centuries. It is twice the size of the largest known bird. (Art by Mark Rollins.)

of such a fate? In fact, menacing giant birds can be found around the world in a record of folklore and events told-as-true.

The Roc and the Thunderbird—fearsome flying creatures of legend—are firmly fixed today as figures in myth and as familiar names in popular culture. The Roc was the most spectacular creature in the tales of the Arabian Nights. It was said to carry off large animals and people. The Thunderbird was said to do the same in the Americas. In ancient Sumeria, the Imgig carried off antelopes. In New Zealand, the Poua-kai was a monster bird. These are all legendary creatures. But could they once have possessed a greater reality, that of living giant birds?

Fossil finds by paleontologists have described the hardened remains of monster birds known to have existed in the past. The finds show that human beings may once have been prey to such flying wonders. There may be truth in the ancient tales, the primitive rock art, and the oral heritage passed through generations of peoples scattered around the world.

But could that reality be manifested today? Is there something to the modern sightings, the reports of strange birds discounted by ornithologists, and the alleged photographs that supposedly show extraordinary winged creatures? People living today have claimed to have experienced the menace told of in folklore—that of being grasped by a winged monster and taken into the air. We will examine their experience, the folklore, the fact, and the menace that contribute to mankind's overlooked natural history. The consideration of all these questions will take us around the globe and through centuries of mankind's experiences.

We begin with one particular story that emerged from the events of a Midwestern town in 1977.

Countless news items reach the American people every day over radio and television waves, on the Internet, and in the pages of newspapers. On July 28, 1977, the news included a story from central Illinois: a ten-year-old boy said he had been lifted into the air by a giant bird.

The story was broadcast on radio and printed in newspapers, including the front pages in St. Louis and Detroit, and more reports of large birds were carried on subsequent days. Within a week, a chorus of remarks belittling all such reports arose from ornithologists and wildlife personnel in Illinois. They said the excitement was caused by mere turkey vultures, common birds with a wingspan no greater than 6 feet (1.8 meters). Because birds are incapable of lifting the weight of a ten-year-old boy, they said it didn't happen. Following these statements, attention to reports of giant birds nearly disappeared.

But much more can be said about this particular news item. In fact, the experience of one ten-year-old boy in the summer of 1977 has an important place in a long historical record of mankind's reported encounters with giant birds.

To backtrack a bit, the experience began in the warm, humid evening hours of Monday, July 25, 1977. Three boys were playing hide-and-seek in the yard of a home in Lawndale, in Logan County, Illinois. [4] Travis Goodwin, Michael Thompson, and ten-year-old Marlon Lowe were in the backyard of the Lowe home when, at 8:30 p.m., two birds approached from the south. Marlon Lowe later told Rick Baker of the Bloomington *Pantagraph* [5] that the three boys saw the birds swoop down toward Travis Goodwin. His friend ran away from the birds and leaped into a small swimming pool in the yard. The birds then headed for Marlon, and the next thing he knew they were right over him. One bird picked him up by the straps of his sleeveless shirt and lifted him about 2 feet (60 centimeters) off the ground. As the bird carried the boy's 65-pound (30-kilogram) weight, Marlon screamed for his mother and punched at the bird. The bird dropped him to the ground after flying 35 or 40 feet (10.6 or 12 meters) from the backyard to the frontyard.

In response to the boy's screams, four adults came on the scene. Marlon's parents, Ruth and Jake Lowe, and two friends from Lincoln, Betty and Jim Daniels, were cleaning out a camper parked in the Lowe's driveway. As Marlon yelled "Mom! Mom!" Mrs. Lowe emerged in time to see her son being carried 2 feet (60 centimeters) off the ground by a bird, a bird she thought had an 8- or 10-foot (2.4 or 3-meter) wingspan. "He was hitting at it with his fists. If he hadn't it never would have dropped him," she told Larry Finley of the Chicago *Daily News*. [6] According to Ruth Lowe, "the birds just cleared the top of the camper, went beneath some telephone wires and flapped their wings—very gracefully—one more time. I was backing up because they got very close to me." [7]

Following Mrs. Lowe, the other adults appeared in time to observe the birds fly off to the north in the direction of some large trees that grow along Kickapoo Creek. That was the last they saw of the birds.

From this experience, those present consistently described both birds as entirely black except for a white ring on their long necks. The beaks were large and curved downward. Ruth Lowe, who had the best look at the birds among the adults, thought the birds might be as much as 4 feet (1.2 meters) in length and might possess wingspans of 8 to 10 feet (2.4 to 3 meters). Estimates of the wingspans varied as might be expected in the circumstances of the birds' sudden and brief appearance and the difficulty of guessing the wingspan of any bird in flight. In light of subsequent reports made in better circumstances, it's possible that the wingspan here is underestimated.

Following his release from the bird's talons, Marlon Lowe

ran into the camper in the Lowe driveway and wouldn't come out for a long while. Reportedly he wasn't even scratched from the experience. His shirt was frayed but not torn. His mother reported that afterward he spent a restless night trying to sleep. "He kept fighting those birds all night long," she said.

That evening, Mrs. Lowe called the police and a game warden because of her concern for other children who swim and fish at Kickapoo Creek, toward which the birds had been seen flying. Logan County sheriff deputies were reported to have searched the area on July 25 and 26. Presumably, they saw nothing, since no findings were reported.

For her concern, Ruth Lowe received a response not unusual for persons reporting something previously unheard of—harsh ridicule. The report to the police inevitably resulted in newspaper stories and other publicity, and then crank phone calls. Mrs. Lowe told Dan Tackett of the Lincoln *Courier* [8] that "people are calling Marlon 'the little bird boy.' They ask if we've caught the birds yet, then hang up. Or, they want to know what we've been drinking." She said on the evening of July 27 they received six such calls in the space of only 45 minutes. She called the police out of her feeling of a citizen's responsibility to report something potentially dangerous, but she eventually concluded, "If I had to do it over again, I wouldn't tell a soul."

The statements of another adult witness to the event of July 25 may well be explained in the light of this extreme reaction by some of the public. James Daniels, who saw the birds fly off, told what he witnessed to Steve Hahn of the Springfield *State Journal-Register*. [9] He saw the birds from 15 feet (4.6 meters) away as they rose from about 6 feet (1.8 meters) above the ground and flew down the street toward Kickapoo Creek. In this account he marveled at the creatures, saying, "I've been around this planet 51 years and I've never seen anything like it." He gave an estimate of 8 feet (2.4 meters) for the wingspan and 4 feet (1.2 meters) for the length of the birds. He noticed white fuzz around the necks and wingtips.

Daniels told Dan Tackett of the Lincoln *Courier*, "They looked like overgrown vultures." [10] Later, however, according to the Pekin *Daily Times*, [11] he changed his account, saying the wingspan was closer to 4 feet (1.2 meters) or a little better, and he was—according to the paper—"definite that the wingspans were nothing even close to 8 feet [2.4 meters]. Perhaps the changes in James Daniels' recollection were motivated by the unsubtle pressure of ridicule and harsh statements that followed quickly after the initial report.

Even local wildlife officials were unrestrained and immediately denied the story was true. A Logan County conservation officer, A.A. Mervar, was quoted as saying, "I don't think the child was picked up." [12] Vern Wright, a biologist with the Illinois Department of Conservation in Springfield, told the press the flying creature definitely did not pick up the boy. [13] (The full extent and impact of such comments will be examined in chapter 3.)

Witnesses to a strange event can only relate what they have seen and cannot be expected to explain it. Still, in this case, Ruth Lowe made a considerable effort to identify the kind of bird she had seen. Conservation officer Mervar brought photos for her to examine, including the common turkey vulture. None of the photos matched her memory of it. Ruth Lowe also spent two hours at the Lincoln Public Library on July 27 trying to find a photograph similar to the birds she saw. She came away convinced she had seen California condors. According to Mrs. Lowe, her son picked out two photos of condors as the culprit birds. And Michael Thompson, present in the yard during the event, picked the same two photos. [14] California condors are nearly extinct vultures found in the wild, and until 1987 only in the vicinity of southern California. They aren't considered to be capable of lifting heavy animals or even inclined to seek live prey. In addition, their colors are not those of the birds described in Illinois, and they simply are not recognized as attaining the size of the Illinois birds. Probably, among all the known birds, they looked most like the Lawndale monsters. The physical description and lifting ability of the Lawndale birds simply do not match recognized birds from anywhere.

The Lowes and others present did no more than report something that was unfamiliar to people around them. Such a report is not unfamiliar to those people who pursue stories of strange animals. In fairness to the people who are by chance recent witnesses to these birds, no action by the Lowes or anything said about them in public raised any doubts about the family's credibility. And in response to the remarks harshly leveled at her family, Ruth Lowe said flatly, "I don't drink and I don't lie. I want people to know that." [15]

The incident at Lawndale didn't present the most desirable description of the birds involved. None of the witnesses offered an estimate of the duration of the animals' presence, but from their accounts, the birds could have come and gone within one or two minutes, and they were in constant motion the whole time.

The record of this event suggests that something extraordinary did happen. And the testimonies of Ruth Lowe and young Marlon Lowe are firm in their assertion that the boy was picked up and carried a distance by a bird resembling an extraordinary vulture. Fortunately for our understanding of this event, birds of the same description were soon reported again.

CHAPTER 2

They Are Seen Again

THE RIDICULE SUFFERED BY THE LOWES FOLLOWING their report didn't keep all citizens of Illinois from declaring to news gatherers and some legal authorities that they too were seeing large birds during July and August of 1977. News of the Lowe incident prompted people to make known both previous and subsequent sightings of birds that puzzled them. Residents became sensitive to various large birds in their vicinity, not just the giant type. Peafowl, turkey vultures, and great blue herons—as well as some truly unfamiliar birds—were the subjects of newspaper stories during this period.

A family in New Holland, Illinois, to the west of Lawndale, spoke up about having seen a strange bird at their farm on July 22. Following the Lowe report, Norma and Kenneth Knollenberg gave a detailed description and even provided a photograph of a turkey-sized bird perched on their barn. Kenneth Knollenberg pointed out that their bird didn't match the Lawndale ones, but he suggested that perhaps their strange bird and the Lawndale birds had all escaped from the same place, such as a zoo or a traveling show.

The Knollenberg's description and photograph indicated the bird was a peahen. [1] This specimen was probably among some loose peafowl reported by construction workers at nearby Middleton. Those birds were thought to have originated with a tame group of peafowl kept by a landowner in Corwin Township. [2]

On July 28, the third day after the Lowe experience, Janet Brandt of Armington, Illinois, was driving home on the Minier-to-Armington road. At 5:30 p.m., she noticed a bird larger than the hood of her car, flying east to west at rooftop level. She had this bird in sight only briefly but did notice a ring of white on its neck. [3]

At 8:00 p.m. of the same day, six people at Stanley Thompson's farm near Covell in McLean County observed a flying enigma. They had been watching model planes flown by radio-control when a living creature appeared, possibly attracted by the novel aerial show. It seemed about to land on the Thompson barn when the startled observers began to yell, "It's a bird!" Apparently

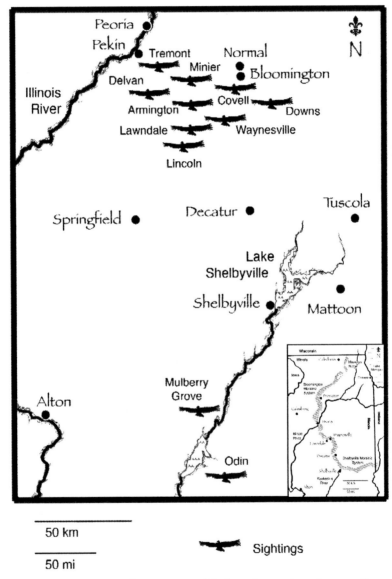

Thunderbird sightings in Illinois. Reports fall along the moraines shown on the inset map. (Art by Mark Rollins.)

THUNDERBIRDS

disturbed by this shouting, the bird then circled and flew off toward Bloomington in graceful flight. It remained visible for a long time due to its size, according to Mrs. Thompson. Stanley Thompson estimated its body was 6 feet (1.8 meters) long and its wingspan was 9 or 10 feet (2.7 or 3 meters). The bird's coloring was brown with white wing tips. [4]

As the sun set on this same Thursday, July 28, Lisa Montgomery, 18 years old, was washing her car in Tremont when she looked up to see one large bird soaring slowly over a cornfield. It looked black with a "real low tail." Her guess put the wingspan at 6 or 7 feet (1.8 or 2.1 meters). She lost sight of it when it flew toward Pekin, in the direction of the setting sun. [5]

The three reports for this date were all in Tazewell and McLean counties of Illinois, directly to the north of Logan County, the location of Lawndale. While the three reports resemble the Lawndale episode, other bird reports at the time of the ongoing extraordinary activity continued to muddle any clear perception. A fourth bird report was made on July 28 at 8:30 p.m. south of Lincoln. In this case, a large, crane-like bird was reported to Logan County police, who withheld the names of the four witnesses due to the sad experience of harassment to the Lowe family. The description was too poor to identify this bird with certainty. [6] The comparison with a crane doesn't sound like vulture-like birds. During the evening of August 3, people playing softball observed a large crane-like bird beside Memorial Park in Lincoln. [7] These birds near Lincoln may well have been herons. Herons were definitely responsible for reports elsewhere, and before the end of July the two giant birds were being reported far away from Logan County, as further reports will indicate.

On Friday, July 29, another predatory act of a giant bird was reported, this time by James Majors, a mailman from Bloomington, Illinois. At 5:50 a.m., he was driving his truck from Armington to Delavan past a Hampshire hog farm in Tazewell County. He braked at the sight of two large birds in the sky. He watched as one stayed high in the air and the other flew low over a cornfield, extending its legs more than two feet (60 centimeters) below its body. Its claws closed on what Majors thought was a baby pig. He guessed the pig's weight at 40 to 60 pounds (18 to 27 kilograms). Majors compared the sound of the bird's flapping wings to the noise of "a jet taking off." The bird crossed the road in front of his truck, getting within 30 to 40 feet (9 to 12 meters) of him. The birds then joined and flew to the north.

Majors was the sole witness to this event. He gave the following descriptive traits for the predator he saw: wingspan of 8 feet (2.4 meters) or larger, plump belly, straight tail, legs and claws totaling 2.5 to 3.5 feet (76 centimeters to 1 meter) long, a bill 6 to 8 inches (152 to 203 millimeters) long, and a "mean-looking" appearance. Majors had seen condors in California and said that the Illinois birds were larger. [8]

The weekend arrived, and bird sightings were many as the residents of Illinois relaxed and carefully observed their surroundings, possibly looking eagerly for the birds that had been in the news all week.

On Saturday at 2:00 a.m., Dennis Turner of Downs, Illinois, and two friends weren't disappointed. Near Gillum, in south-central McLean County, they saw perched on a telephone pole a bird they thought had a 6-foot (1.8-meter) wingspan. They observed the bird dropping an object near the pole. Later, police found a foot-long (30-centimeter) rat at the spot. [9]

Later still in the morning hours of July 30, another incident took place, and unique evidence was obtained to support the account given. That morning "Texas John" Huffer, an outdoor writer from Tuscola, Illinois, was fishing along with his son on Lake Shelbyville. This reservoir covers 11,100 acres (4495.5 hectares) along the Kaskaskia and Okaw rivers and is located about 60 miles (96.5 kilometers) southeast of Lawndale.

The Huffers were fishing in a boat in a secluded bay at the north end of the lake when they took an interest in two birds perched in a tree. The sound of their boat horn sent the birds flying. The larger of the two birds flew from one tree to another as the Huffers followed in their boat. The smaller bird disappeared. Huffer had a motion film camera with him. He had years of experience filming in the wild and had seen service as a combat photographer in the Marines. He shot 100 feet of color film of this strange bird. He estimated that the wingspan was 12 feet (3.6 meters). The bird was black and made a kind of clacking sound.

Huffer thought its cry was "primeval."

A new wrinkle to the bird stories, but admittedly a logical find, was reported by Huffer. Beneath a tree where the birds had perched, he found balls of dung the size of baseballs. As might be expected, this item was treated humorously in newspapers. The film was aired on a Champaign television station the same day it was filmed. [10] (This film is discussed further in chapter 12.)

At 2:00 p.m. on the same Saturday of the Huffer report, residents of Waynesville in DeWitt County reported a large black bird with an 8-foot (2.4-meter) wingspan. The bird seemed to be looking for a place to land, but did not. [11] This report placed one bird 60 miles (96.5 kilometers) to the northwest of Lake Shelbyville after two birds were seen there hours earlier. The time of day is unique—other accounts of strange birds took place in early morning and early evening hours, with one sighting in the middle of the night.

Unfortunately, no witnesses were named; only "residents" were credited with making a sighting. The press had become reluctant to name witnesses.

Reports of birds were made in the vicinity of Bloomington the next day, Sunday, July 31, and newspapers covered them. A teenager, Albert Dunham II, filmed the birds as they flew over his home around 4:00 p.m. on Sunday. It was reported that a neighbor tried to use a tranquilizer gun to capture the bird. Young Dunham followed the bird to a local landfill. Bob Ringham, a *Pantagraph* photographer, went in search of this bird and learned from a local resident that three crane-like birds had been frequenting the landfill for three years. [12] The birds turned out to be great blue herons, which can be elusive but are not unusual. [13]

On Monday, August 1, Illinois went back to work. Another summer weekend was history, and so were the sightings of giant birds. The newspapers were discussing great blue herons and the "bird experts" were sure that nothing unusual was being seen over Illinois. It must have seemed to many that the entire story was another "nine days' wonder," or something that causes a great sensation for a few days and then passes into the limbo of things forgotten. This phrase has been traced back to an old proverb that implies that the public is similar to newborn kittens and puppies, which are born temporarily blind. And "the eyes of the public are blind in astonishment for nine days, but then their eyes are open, and they see too much to wonder any longer." [14]

When another giant bird was reported on August 11, 1977, the event was hardly noticed. The community of Odin is about 60 miles (96.5 kilometers) south of Lake Shelbyville. A family near Odin observed a bird for five to 10 minutes with the aid of binoculars. The local daily newspaper, the Centralia *Sentinel*, carried their story the same day it was reported—albeit on page 8. The next day the Chicago *Sun-Times* carried a three-paragraph dispatch from United Press International—on page 12. The Chicago *Tribune* had a similarly brief version of the UPI dispatch on August 15. No other press mention of this story has been found, yet these observations were the most detailed of the entire series of strange bird stories in 1977.

John Chappell of Odin told UPI that a gray-black bird arrived at the Chappell farm from the northeast at about seven in the morning of August 11. The bird then circled above their small pond and came to rest in a tree. He thought the bird was "so big it had a hard time finding a limb big enough to land on." From a distance of 400 feet (122 meters), he estimated the wingspan of the creature was 10 to 12 feet (3 to 3.6 meters) and that the body was 6 feet (1.8 meters) long. The distance from the "top of the beak to the back of the head" was 8 inches (203 millimeters). [15]

John Chappell's wife, Wanda, was interviewed at length by

the Centralia *Sentinel*. The Chappell farm, it was reported, is three miles (4.8 kilometers) south of Odin. The morning of the sighting, the Chappells were having coffee and looking through a sliding glass door toward their pond. The bird flew in and circled 300 to 400 feet (91.4 to 122 meters) away. Wanda Chappell was familiar with buzzards and said this bird was so big "there was no comparison," and "when it settled in the tree, the tree settled quite a bit" so she knew it was heavy. They were careful not to open the sliding door because they did not want to scare it away. They called their son, John, who also observed the bird. They did not awaken their year-and-a-half-old daughter.

The bird remained for five to 10 minutes. Mrs. Chappell used binoculars to watch it. Judging by the length of a 16-foot (4.9-meter) boat on the pond, she thought its wingspan was 14 feet (4.2 meters). It appeared to be 4 feet (1.2 meters) high. She gave these further details: "It looked like a prehistoric bird. It was really fantastic. The head didn't have any feathers and it had a long neck, crooked, kind of 'S' shaped. The body was covered with feathers and was gray or charcoal-colored. We couldn't tell much about the feet, but it had long legs."

The Chappells didn't hear the creature make any noise. Wanda thought it resembled an enormous vulture and was big enough to carry off a child older than her daughter. When the bird flew off, it went southwest toward Raccoon Lake and the town of Centralia, which ended the last of the year's giant-bird reports. [16]

The description of events in Illinois in 1977 has been drawn from what is generally thought of as the "public record," in this case, statements of ordinary people taken down by people who write for newspapers. As shown here, when they're brought together, they contain extraordinary claims of giant birds said to seek and carry off large prey; they contain contradictions such as James Daniels' statements about the Lowe sighting; and they indicate some disagreement about details among witnesses to the same event, as in the dimensions of the bird at the Chappell farm. But when the likes of the peafowl and great blue herons are set aside, nine incidents remain that contribute, however unevenly in minor specifics, to a logical series of events that can be reconstructed.

Two large birds, one clearly larger than the other, made their first reported appearance at Lawndale on a Monday; this is the Lowe sighting. The following Thursday, Friday, and Saturday, at least one or both were reported five times in a triangular area of 330 square miles (855 square kilometers). The area is bounded by Lawndale, Tremont, and Downs (the Brandt, Thompson, Montgomery, Majors, and Turner sightings). This area is drained mainly by Kickapoo and Sugar creeks and in the northwest by the Mackinaw River.

The reports indicate they were seeking a large meal the size of a ten-year-old boy and more than the size of a baby pig or a rat. The absence of any wild prey in this populated area is likely to be why a human being was attacked. Leaving behind the rejected rat, the birds appear to have flown 60 miles (96.5 kilometers) south to Lake Shelbyville in the early morning hours of Saturday. There the birds were disturbed by the boat-horn of T.J. Huffer and the birds split up. While Huffer filmed the larger one, the other may have started north to their previous haunt, where it may have been seen on Saturday afternoon at Waynesville. Twelve days after the Huffer sighting, the big one had followed the outlet of Lake Shelbyville, the Kaskaskia River, southwestward to the vicinity of Odin. After a pause at the Chappell farm, it continued its exit from central Illinois—alone.

Wanda Chappell admitted to being hesitant to report her observation of the giant bird, but, when she called her sister in Alma, Illinois, she heard that the bird had been seen the previous day. She thought others might make sightings known. [17] But whoever had seen the thing that earlier day didn't come forward, and no other reports were forthcoming. Giant bird reports had tumbled quickly into the limbo of the forgotten. To see why this happened, we next examine what takes place when people claim to have seen a monster— and how modern America reacted when the menace of giant birds appeared in her heartland.

CHAPTER 3

Another Nine-Day Wonder

RUTH LOWE WAITED TWO HOURS BEFORE CALLING the police to tell them of her experience. "I thought if I tell the police they'll think I'm crazy, and they did," she later observed. [1] Mrs. Lowe was not prepared, however, for the crank calls and official comments that came from Springfield to Chicago. "But," she said, "some people called to say they did believe me. Yet I don't expect officials to stand there and tell me that I didn't see it." [2] Officials did just that. And the comments from assorted experts and the ways the various news media cover a nine-day wonder often are important to understanding the emergence and disappearance of the entire episode.

In the nine days from July 26 to August 3, 1977, the wonder of the nation was "big birds" in the state of Illinois. Publicity began with the call to the police, and local Illinois daily papers then publicized the story with staff-written articles.

The Lowe report on Monday night made its very first press appearance in the Lincoln *Courier* the next afternoon on page 10. While the *Courier* is a member of the Associated Press, meaning AP may circulate the paper's stories, no resulting AP dispatches were found. On Wednesday morning, the *State Register-Journal* in Springfield put the story at the top of page 1. The Bloomington *Pantagraph* ran its first story on Wednesday on page A-11.

In 1977, Chicago was home to three influential newspapers—the Tribune, the *Daily News*, and the *Sun-Times*—whose stories were routinely syndicated to other papers around the country. The *News* ran a staff-written piece on page 18 of its final Red Streak Edition on Wednesday, and put the same story the next day in its State Edition on page 7. On Thursday, newspapers from Massachusetts to Florida to Texas had the story in a United Press

International dispatch. The *Sun-Times* then joined the *News* in covering the "big bird" events. UPI, which is the principal wire service in competition with the Associated Press, became the one constant source of bird news throughout the period, right up to the last report near Odin.

The daily papers of central Illinois—in Bloomington-Normal, Champaign-Urbana, Decatur, Lincoln, Mattoon, Pekin, Peoria, and Springfield—all tried to follow the bird saga with staff-written articles or, when unable to interview witnesses themselves, with UPI dispatches. Ruth Lowe must have been a most patient woman at the end of July because the public record indicates she was interviewed by the Lincoln *Courier*, the Springfield *State Journal-Register*, the Chicago *Daily News*, the Bloomington *Pantagraph*, the Decatur *Herald*, UPI, and an unknown number of radio and television people.

Not all the media embraced the bird stories quickly. The Chicago *Tribune* introduced its readers to the story only on Saturday, July 30. The headline on page 3 read: "Expert: 'Attack' Tale is for the Birds." The first paragraph of this staff-written article consisted of two words: "Thoroughly ridiculous!" On August 1 or 2, depending on the edition, the newspaper found space for a UPI dispatch on the Huffer film. On August 4 and August 15, the story was covered in two small wire service reports that, taken together, totaled six paragraphs.

This writer heard directly from one newspaper editor whose office was 5 miles (8 kilometers) from a sighting of the birds. He wrote: "Our only comment is that August is the silly season. Look out for flying saucers chasing the big birds."

On August 3, the "nine days" of the old axiom were up, and the story, for most people, dropped out of sight. The push was provided by the Associated Press, which had less liking for big birds than even the Chicago *Tribune*. While UPI and many Illinois journalists were busy reporting bird stories, those persons at the AP who decide what news will circulate to AP members clearly decided against the latest wonder. Until August 3, the only mention by the AP came when an African stork escaped from the Brookfield, Illinois, zoo on July 30. An AP dispatch widely printed on August 1 contained this passage: "The escape came amid rumors from central Illinois of a large, mysterious bird that swoops down and grabs children. But zoo keepers scoffed at the notion that the big stork or any other bird could lift a 70-pound [31.8-kilogram] child, as one woman reported." [3]

Two days later, the wonder tumbled into limbo when the AP finally found some big bird news it wanted to circulate. From Springfield came a dispatch with the opinions of three men identified as wildlife experts who, with terms such as "turkey vultures," "impossible," and "hysteria," dismissed everything that had been reported. This dispatch ended the previously widespread interest.

With the competition at the time between the press and radio to report the latest bird sightings, radio's use of this AP story was probably enough to finish off the wonder. The publication of the AP item was rare in Illinois itself. A search of the state's newspapers found that only the Chicago *Tribune* carried three paragraphs of it on August 4 ("Giant Winged Bird Just a Turkey Vulture"). [4] Newspapers just outside the state were more inclined to publish long versions of the denunciations by the AP sources; these appeared in the St. Louis (Missouri) *Globe-Democrat* ("Big Bird Turns Out to be for the Birds") and in the Des Moines (Iowa) *Register* ("Experts 'Talk Turkey' on Big Bird Story"). [5] As noted earlier, when the Chappells made their report eight days later, the people of Illinois, let alone the country, hardly noticed.

The record of reporting shows that the Illinois "big birds" were not an overnight sensation. The first report took three days to become widely known. Only then did other reports surface. Interest was high into the following weekend. But stories effectively ceased after the AP broke what amounted to a news blackout on the subject with a totally negative discussion of the witnesses and their reports. The last report couldn't revive the previous interest, and the

AP's "experts" seemed to have the last word on the subject.

The news media provided more than straight reporting on the wonder. Something of a competition developed to coin a catchy moniker for the birds. The obvious "Big Bird" competed with "King Vulture," "King Condor," and "Bigclaw." A radio station in Bloomington offered a $500 reward for any live bird with a wingspan of 7 feet (2.1 meters) or more. [6] As a sign of the economic times, the Des Moines *Register* ran a political cartoon on page 1 showing an astounded "economic expert" being lifted in the claws of a giant bird called "the new inflation." [7]

Suddenly, during the period of the nine-day wonder, any bird story was important. One paper even ran a photograph of a turkey vulture that apparently was wounded by a hunter in Tuscarora Township the previous November. [8] Much print was given to the Marabou stork that escaped from the Brookfield Zoo on July 30. This bird flew north 70 miles (113 kilometers) into Wisconsin, where it was shot from a tree with a tranquilizer dart. The fall of 70 feet (21.3 meters) to the ground injured the bird so much it soon died. [9] The superintendent of birds at the Brookfield Zoo, Dennis DeCourcey, took the opportunity to comment that "no bird ever existed that could carry away a child—impossible." [10]

People supposed by the press to be expert in ornithology or Illinois wildlife had a lot to say about what other people were seeing in Illinois. No less than ten such people other than DeCourcey were quoted on the topic of what birds had been seen at Lawndale.

Vern Wright, a biologist with the Illinois Department of Conservation, thought witnesses at Lawndale saw large birds but that the boy was not picked up. He couldn't identify the birds, but speculated they were turkey vultures or black vultures. [11] A.A. Mervar, the Logan County conservation officer, ignored the multiple witnesses when he suggested the boy was scared and only thought he was picked up. Mervar thought some kind of vulture was seen near the boys and said, "I don't think the child was picked up." [12]

John Borneman, a National Audubon Society naturalist, was contacted in Ventura, California, for his knowledge of condors. He affirmed that condors were not sighted outside of California and nearby Mexico. "Condors are shy of people, they would never swoop down," he added. Another point against condors is that they always roost by dusk and do not fly late in the day. Borneman suggested that great horned owls or trained hawks would swoop down on people. [13]

William Beecher, an ornithologist and director of the Chicago Academy of Sciences-Museum of Ecology, declared that the reports were ridiculous and that "in the whole history of the world there never has been a bird capable of carrying a 65-pound [29.5 kilogram] load." He cited the relatively small weights of known birds—the condor, the bald eagle, and the turkey vulture—and dismissed them as being involved. [14]

James Karr, an associate professor of ecology at the University of Illinois, expressed himself with zeroes: zero possibility of a condor and zero possibility of a bird picking up a boy or a pig. [15]

Former game warden Leo Borgelt was puzzled and said he was waiting to see what turned up. He and another conservation officer, Wally Litwiller of Hopedale, thought the birds were most likely turkey vultures. [16]

The statements of three experts were used when the Associated Press lowered the boom on the "rumors" the AP had ignored but which had kept their competitors busy. Beecher was contacted, and he obliged with these comments: "What we're seeing is a lot of hysteria. . . . There are a lot of turkey vultures in that area, but a lot of people may not see them very often."

Jack Ellis, a supervisor of wildlife resources for the Illinois Department of Conservation, and George Kulesza, an ornithologist at the University of Illinois, both made their statements to AP after viewing the Huffer film. Ellis said flatly the birds were turkey vultures. Kulesza said, "One can never be 100 percent certain, but it seems to me highly unlikely that it could be anything else [other than turkey vultures]." Ellis called the report of bird droppings the size of baseballs impossible, citing his knowledge of turkey vulture droppings. [17]

The last expert received notice in *Outdoor Highlights*, a publication of the Illinois Department of Conservation. The August 8, 1977, issue reported on the DOC's non-game biologist, Vernon Kleen, who had been assigned to "solve the mystery." He was "traveling Logan County . . . in an effort to view, photograph, and identify the creature." Kleen had seen the Huffer film and thought it showed turkey vultures. He was inclined to think the Logan County birds also were buzzards. The article concluded: "Kleen believes the birds were young vultures. Because of their youth, they couldn't fly high, as adult vultures do. When the birds and boy found themselves in proximity to each other, they all panicked and in their efforts to escape they may all have headed in the same direction. The facts should be known soon." [18] This writer wrote to Vernon Kleen in August 1977 but didn't receive a reply.

Supposed experts bring limited knowledge to bear when a question such as living giant birds arises. They are keepers of the commonplace and the familiar, and they consider all questions within such a framework. The lack of knowledge on the part of Illinois' 11 bird experts was most evident when no one mentioned the state's history of giant bird sightings.

The following is a news dispatch for April 9 from Belvidere, which is located in Boone County in northern Illinois:

A farmer and a truck driver reported today that
they had seen a bird "bigger than an airplane."
The giant bird was reported by Robert Price and
Veryl Babb. Price said he saw it when working
near his barn on his farm near Caledonia, Illinois.
He said it had a long neck and "what I suppose
were its feet trailing behind it." Price said he and

his wife both watched as the "monster bird," flapping its powerful wings, flew off up to the northeast. Babb, a Freeport truck driver, reported seeing the bird at a different location on the same day. "I did see the bird, but at first I didn't say anything because I thought people would laugh at me," Babb said. "When I read that Price had seen it I decided to report all about it."

This familiar-sounding news was reported by United Press in the year 1948. [19]

From January to early May 1948, the Midwest experienced sightings of giant birds. These sightings weren't centered in northern Illinois, as with the Price and Babb reports. Neither were they in central Illinois, as in 1977. Most of them occurred around Alton, Illinois, near St. Louis, and in parts of Missouri close to St. Louis and Alton.

The dispatch from Belvidere prompted readers of the St. Louis *Post-Dispatch* to say that they were seeing something right around St. Louis. The family of a 12-year-old boy declared their son had said that he saw a giant bird, gray-green in color, over their home in Overland, Missouri, in January. In addition, a former Army colonel, Walter F. Siegmund, saw an enormous bird flying northeast over Alton on April 4. That month, reports continued over Alton, Overland, and St. Louis. Typically, the bird was compared to a Piper Cub airplane and appeared dark gray in color. Witnesses reported thinking they were seeing an airplane until the creature flapped its wings. One observer, E.M. Coleman of Alton, insisted the bird fit the description of a condor in every way.

Charles Hartenstein, an assistant to the mayor of St. Louis, was assigned the task of trapping the "what-is-it" or "big bird," as it was alternately labeled. He announced he would let it come to him since he had no airplane. Money going further in those days, a reward of only ten dollars was offered by one Harry Bradford, who wanted not the bird but merely a "plausible explanation" for something he had seen three times in four days. None came. [20]

If the bird experts of 1977 had heard of the 1948 happenings, they couldn't bring themselves to say so when the press—for a few days—was eager for every angle on the bird stories. But such information is not the stock in trade of ornithologists and wildlife specialists such as state offices provide. These people have jobs with specific and routine duties and, most especially, with status. This last characteristic brings pressure from peers and one's public image as an "expert." And, as writer Charles Fort (1874-1932) observed many years ago, experts fear more than anything else being obviously baffled. [21]

The task of patiently sorting through the clamorous results of a nine-day wonder falls to dedicated amateur non-experts, who are not paid to investigate anything but do so anyway. They are followers—in a way—in the footsteps of the author Charles Fort, who gathered unexplained data from the scientific journals of his day and put them into his books. Such "non-experts" take time away from their professions to search for and research mysteries. And they find a lot to do.

Loren Coleman is such a person. In 1979, he visited the Lowe family and confirmed the facts of the Lawndale incident as reported in the press. He also discovered the depth of the human cost of a nine-day wonder. Coleman learned that the Lowe family had been harrassed with phone calls, notes, and, especially, dead birds of all kinds constantly deposited on their porch. And a month after the famous incident, Mrs. Lowe discovered that her son's previously red hair had taken on a gray coloring permanently.

Coleman also found that giant bird reports were still being made in Illinois. A mobile home park at Belleville near St. Louis was the landing site of a bird with an 18-foot (5.5-meter) wingspan. News of this occurrence came from Ruth Lowe's sister-in-law, who lived at the park. [22]

The final word on the Illinois wonder deservedly goes to

Ruth Lowe. After all the experts had their say, Mrs. Lowe, who spoke from personal experience, has made the most perceptive comment on the appearance of two extraordinary birds in Illinois. She was quoted as saying: "The game warden said there wasn't anything like this ever reported in the county. Maybe there wasn't, but there is now. Two came through here last night." [23]

The experiences such as those of 1948 and 1977 take place in a context unknown to the usual "experts." The so-called experts look only for common and familiar animals or mistakes and hoaxes. But animals can be rare and elusive. Some, perhaps, must avoid mankind to survive. So we find among the collections of those followers of Charles Fort—known ever more frequently as "forteans"—abundant knowledge of giant birds.

From the nine-day-wonder of 1977 and the reports of giant birds still emerging in the 21st century, we will now move on to explore these in their proper context—the record of centuries of contact between humans and these giant birds.

CHAPTER 4

Birds That Carry Off People

THE EVENTS OF JULY 1977 ARE NOT UNIQUE. GIANT birds had appeared and threatened people before then. The danger to people in our historical era has been too infrequent for the birds to be widely recognized as a menace to the general public.

The first writer to recognize the modern record of giant birds and their extraordinary preying upon human beings was Jack Pearl. In May 1963, Pearl published an article in a widely circulated men's true-adventure magazine called *Saga*. The article was titled "Monster Bird That Carries Off Human Beings!" In it, Pearl related stories from the 18th to the 20th centuries that he thought told of appearances of the Thunderbird in North America. This bird was a feature of American Indian legends about storms and powerful sky spirits. Pearl's stories have since been repeated by other writers and have been influential in fanning a modern interest in giant birds.

Pearl wrote that frontiersman Daniel Boone and scout Jim Bridger both had encounters with giant birds.

> The famous scout Jim Bridger described how a "giant bird, too big for either an eagle or a vulture," attacked a tethered mule and lifted it off the ground. Bridger and a companion held onto the animal's legs, and eventually the bird loosened its grip and flew away.
>
> Daniel Boone claimed to have seen a Thunderbird carry away a five-year-old Indian boy. A dozen arrows and a volley of shots were supposedly pumped into the creature without effect. [1]

While such stories might appear in the lore of these men, their value is questionable. Pearl noted that "campfire tales . . . cannot be taken too seriously."

Pearl then penned a small paragraph that has since caused an extensive and continuing search for a photograph of a Thunderbird. He stated as a matter fact that a photograph existed in 1886 showing a bird with a 36-foot (11-meter) wingspan nailed to a wall. Such a picture would be remarkable indeed. (A discussion of this alleged evidence for the Thunderbird is presented in chapter 12.)

Pearl went on to relate an incident supposed to have happened outside Tombstone in the Arizona Territory in 1889. Five saloon drunks spent the night in the desert, and in the morning four of them were awakened by the cries of the fifth calling for help, which then faded away high in the air. That man was not seen again. We are told the remaining four signed sworn statements of their testimony. This little story without names sounds very much like a twice-told tale of a boy who goes to a well to fetch a bucket of water and then disappears into the dark as if carried off by something unknown. This chestnut has been linked to various times and locations but hasn't been found to have a basis in history. Pearl's version sounds like that tale simply dressed up in Western garb.

Advancing to the year 1933, Pearl gave an account from southeastern California, apparently told by a medical doctor. The doctor was summoned from a mining camp near Ivanpah to an isolated farm, where he treated a family of three. The husband, wife, and three-year-old child were all badly cut. The man told of hearing his wife's screams while in his fields. Running to the farmhouse, he found what looked like a giant form of vulture or eagle attacking his wife with beak and claw. One of the creature's wings alone looked to be about 12 feet (3.6 meters) long. The woman defended herself with a stove poker while their child lay between her legs. The husband picked up a nearby axe and struck one telling blow about the shoulder of the bird, causing it to bleed considerably. The bird then lifted the man in its talons 10 feet (3 meters) or more in the air. He was then dropped and the bird flew off, seemingly weakened by loss of blood. The doctor examined the site and found evidence of tremendous bloodletting, more than his patients could account for. So the story went.

According to Pearl, more incidents in 1944 centered on a California internment camp for Japanese-Americans. Internees disappeared and were not heard of again. The camp inhabitants and local Indians both told disbelieving investigators of a monster bird from the mountains that carried people off to their deaths.

Here is how Pearl related these incidents:

> One of the most eerie Thunderbird incidents occurred in 1944, in a California internment camp where Nisei, Americans of Japanese origin, were held during World War II. Over a period of months, more than a half-dozen internees disappeared from this camp, and it was thought they had escaped. In the course of the thorough investigation that followed, to figure out how the Nisei had escaped and who had helped them, the only thing investigators could get out of the internees was that a "giant bird" had carried off the missing men. The angry soldiers assumed that they were being "taken" by the Japanese Americans, who had been fraternizing with local Indians working around the camp. These Indians habitually told wild stories about a monster bird that lurked in the lofty mountain peaks. The opinion was reinforced when two of the Indians rushed into camp one morning, shouting excitedly that they had seen a Thunderbird kill and carry off a man the night before.

Security was beefed up after that incident and searchlights were placed on the camp perimeter. The disappearances appeared to stop. Pearl concluded:

> Usually when Japanese American internees escaped from the camps, they would be picked up again in days or weeks, while trying to sneak in or out of the homes of friends or mingling self-consciously in Chinese sections, hoping they would be accepted by their brother Orientals. It rarely worked.
>
> Strangely, none of the internees who escaped from the camp ever turned up again—during the war or after. They had, literally and figuratively, disappeared into thin air! So claimed their fellow inmates—and the Indians.

Pearl also recounted later sightings. For example, a pilot told of a near collision over Arizona in 1947 with a bird with a wingspan of over 30 feet (9 meters). Another man described as a New York businessman is said to have been flying his Piper Cub up the Hudson River Valley in May 1961. What he thought was another plane turned out to be a giant bird. He got a long look at it because when he attempted to fly away from it, the creature followed the aircraft for ten minutes before winging on its own way.

No names (other than the two frontiersman who were themselves the topics of legends) and no sources were given for these stories. Pearl may have heard of them by word of mouth, which doesn't make them false; it would mean we are unlikely to learn more about them. While some of them may be true, they are unfortunately as yet unsupported by any historical context. Pearl also thought that a certain airplane crash over Maryland in November 1962 was caused by a collision with a giant bird.

Pearl had his own hypothesis about the Indians' experience with Thunderbirds. He referred to the continent-wide traditions that told of monster birds living in the mountains and taking animal prey—including humans. He suggested the birds left their mountainous habitat and sought food in the valleys, where they preyed upon humans when other food was scarce during a period of climatic cooling around 1400AD (actually the "Little Ice Age" from 1430 to 1850). Furthermore, he thought that during the same period of cooling, the American Indians migrated eastward from the northwestern part of the continent. In the mountains (he didn't say which mountains), the Indians fell prey to the birds and got revenge by destroying the predators' nests and young. The Indians, Pearl wrote, described the nests as crude beds of sticks on exposed mountaintops.

Pearl pointed out a similarity with the nesting habits of the California condor, the nearly extinct bird in southern California. Known condors are incapable of the predatory acts described here, but Pearl cited R. J. Young, identified as a California ornithologist, as saying of the condor: "Although many of my colleagues will not agree, I would say it is not only possible but likely that certain of the species which have endured, are great hardy creatures with wingspreads of up to twenty-five feet [7.6 meters]." He thought such birds would be found only in the West.

With the *Saga* article Jack Pearl gave the popular discussion of Thunderbirds a major boost. The author is almost as interesting as the story of the birds. "Jack Pearl" was a pseudonym of Jacques Bain Pearl (1923-1992), a prolific author under various names. I tried to contact him in the late 1980s to discuss Thunderbirds, but I couldn't get him to respond. His life and career were winding down at that time. His later works were mass-market romances written under the name "Stephanie Blake," the last two of which were published in 1988 and 1990. When I contacted him, he may have been unwilling or even unable to recall the particulars of his only contribution to cryptozoology back in 1963. Nevertheless, Pearl encouraged curiosity about sightings of giant birds and the Thunderbird of legend. But the merits of his stories remain difficult to assess.

Other stories based in historical records have also been

found. They present a clear record of names and places when giant birds have menaced human beings in North America for a period going back more than a century. When we look at this record, we find that it was a common explanation to attribute the attacks to the American bald eagle. These accusations have upset those knowledgeable about eagles. They protest that the bald eagle would not attack and attempt to carry off such prey. I certainly agree. Such labels are misidentifications of something much larger than eagles, something that takes large and live prey as a matter of course. Its normal prey would seem to consist of deer and other large mammals.

Continuing scrutiny of the historical record has produced one item from 1892 that does tell of a bald eagle attempting to make off with a human baby. Found by Nick Sucik, this story, when taken at face value, demonstrates the folly of a bird such as the bald eagle attempting to carry away even the smallest child.

Here is that item as published in the *Arizona Champion* for March 10, 1892:

EXCITING RESCUE OF A CHILD THAT HAD BEEN CARRIED OFF

A party of tourists witnessed a strange sight near Taton, N.M., a few days ago. While going by a little house near the road, they heard the frantic screams of a woman. Several of the men ran to the house and found her standing in the door, screaming "My child, my child," and pointing to an outhouse, on top of which sat a big bald eagle with a child about 1 year old in its talons. Before any of the party could shoot, the noise frightened the bird and picking up the child he flapped his enormous wings and started away. The weight of the child however, was almost too much, and it was impossible for him to rise more than 50 feet above the ground.

A Mr. Roberts in the party had a rifle, but feared to shoot, knowing that if the bird was killed the boy would fall to the ground and be dashed to pieces. The half-crazed mother and the party of tourists ran along, keeping as near as the eagle as possible. At last the mother implored Mr. Roberts to shoot the bird. Thinking the boy's death was almost a certainty in any event. Mr. Roberts took careful aim and fired. The eagle gave a scream and began beating the air viciously with one wing, while the other hung useless by its side. It was almost a minute before the strength of the bird gave out, and it began to fall, still holding on the boy in its talons. It came down, slowly circling about and getting lower and lower each time, and at last reached the ground. The mother rushed for her child, but the eagle began to fight, and it was not until the bird had been killed with the butt of the rifle that the child was released.

The talons of the eagle had got well tied up in the child's clothes and this had saved the boy's life. He was black and blue in many places from being beat by the eagle's wing, but was not otherwise hurt. The mother told the tourists that the eagle had been about the house for a long time, and had almost become a pet. It seemed to be much attached to a dog owned by her husband, and spent much of its time near the dog's kennel. A few weeks before the dog had shown symptoms of madness and had been shot. Since then the eagle had seemed very vicious.

THUNDERBIRDS

So, while we cannot declare that such a thing would never be attempted, it appears that such cases would be rare because of the birds' inability to accomplish a snatch. Another caution must be made. As will be discussed in chapter 13, there are particular environmental circumstances in mountainous terrain—demonstrated in Europe—where updrafts will assist birds of prey in lifting a victim.

The North American chronicle of people attacked by gigantic birds begins in the autumn of 1868. The story was preserved by way of a translator's footnote to the English edition of *The Universe* by French naturalist Felix A. Pouchet, published in New York in 1871. The location is Tippah County, which is in the northeastern corner of Mississippi (not in Missouri, as the footnote reads). The complete text of the story, attributed to a teacher, follows:

> A sad casualty occurred at my school a few days ago. The eagles have been very troublesome in the neighborhood for some time past, carrying off pigs, lambs, &c. No one thought that they would attempt to prey upon children; but on Thursday, at recess, the little boys were out some distance from the house, playing marbles, when their sport was interrupted by a large eagle sweeping down and picking up little Jemmie Kenney, a boy of eight years, and flying away with him. The children cried out, and when I got out of the house, the eagle was so high that I could just hear the child screaming. The alarm was given, and from screaming and shouting in the air, &c. the eagle was induced to drop his victim; but his talons had been buried in him so deeply, and the fall was so great, that he was killed—or either would have been fatal. [2]

The earliest newspaper account has been found by Benoit Crevier. It appeared in the Carleton Place (Ontario) *Herald* for July 21, 1886, with the headline "A Heavy Lift for an Eagle." "The 'Bruce Telescope,' of Walkerton [Indiana], says, Washburn Wright, seven years old, was going through a pasture near Mulberry Grove, Illinois, the other day, when a big bald eagle swooped down, grabbed him by the jacket and actually lift[ed] him from the ground. The boy yelled, the clothes ripped, and the boy's father, rushing to the rescue, drove away the king of birds, who wanted to make a Ganymede out of the youth." Crevier added his own note to this story: "There is no way a Bald Eagle (a well known bird species) could lift a seven-year-old child. Impossible. Thus another unknown bird species?"

Crevier turned up another item with a date of May 17, 1888, in the weekly *The Equity* in Bryson, Quebec. The headline was: "Attacked by an Eagle."

> The Ogdensburg [New York] "Journal" says: "On Wednesday, 2nd inst., Georgie the seven-year-old son of George Rickards, of Brier Hill, in this county, was attacked while out in the field by a very large bald eagle. When the boy saw the eagle swooping down upon him, he armed himself with as large a club as he could wield and fought the bird, which continued its efforts to get hold of him with its talons. When first seen by Burton Rickards, an older brother of George, the eagle was endeavoring to pick up the lad. Burton went to the rescue and drove off the eagle.
>
> "Later Burton set a steel trap in the field where there had been thrown some deacon [i.e., adulterated] carcasses and caught the eagle by the middle claw of one of his talons. Some green sticks were cut and ropes obtained, and a most

vigorous fight initiated to capture the eagle alive. When the rope was thrown over his head, he would take it off with his free leg almost in an instant. He would bite off pieces from the green sticks, which were an inch in diameter, and fought a brave and determined battle. He was finally overpowered by superior force and had to succumb. He was captured alive, and is now in possession of Mr. Rickard [sic].

"The fight and capture took place on the farm of Enoch Young, supervisor of Morristown. The eagle is represented to be a very large one. This is the first instance in which one of these voracious birds has attempted to carry off a child in St. Lawrence County."

A detailed account of a child being the apparent victim of giant birds exists for the year 1895. In Webster County, West Virginia, two birds were observed roosting on a high point of land. The birds harassed people and livestock. The disappearance of ten-year-old Landy Junkins on February 1, 1895, was attributed to these giant fowl. (The full record of this period is given in chapter 8.)

Further north, cases of people falling victim to Thunderbirds in Pennsylvania have been alleged. Hiram Cranmer of that state claimed to know that in 1937 a four-year-old girl was carried off in McKean County. And in 1941, the same fate befell a 75-year-old man, Barney Pluff. Also, Cranmer recalled that there had been a Thunderbird scare around Hammersly Fork when he was a boy, when children were kept home from school out of concern for their safety. (The claims of Hiram Carnmer are discussed further in chapter 9, where the extensive history of the birds in Pennsylvania is presented.)

David Jacobsen, in a 1948 book about rumors, listed some stories that were current in the middle of the 20th century. They indicate that such events were being reported while no one gave them credence and no one bothered to preserve a detailed history. He wrote: "Some years ago the New York 'Herald Tribune' reported that in Kentucky a bald eagle lifted a 50-pound [23-kilogram] boy over twenty feet in the air. In Mississippi another eagle was shot, supposedly because the bird, having a 7-foot [2.1-meter] wingspread, flew away with a 50-pound calf. A four-year-old boy was reportedly attacked and lifted off the ground by an eagle in Florida." [3]

The identification of the birds as eagles didn't please their defenders, who displayed their outrage in the pages of *Audubon Magazine* and *Nature Magazine*. In 1936 and 1948, writers expressed their dismay at "fake eagle stories" and accounts of "super eagles." A couple of incidents misrepresented as "eagle attacks" were described. It was implied but not demonstrated that the kind of incidents described here could be explained in the same way. [4]

As we have reviewed here, the next big story of this kind of attack came in Illinois in 1977. Looking back over the century and a half of reports, it would seem that encounters in which a person is harmed occur every 30 to 40 years. At that pace, it's about time for another incident of such a dangerous and dramatic nature. Where might this take place?

The state of vigilance indicated recently in Alaska and in the past in Pennsylvania suggests that people in those areas are the least likely to be victims. The people in places like Illinois and New York appear more likely to be taken unawares and to be victimized. The reason why residents of those states are vulnerable can be found in the habits of these giant birds. But before we examine their habits in chapter 10, we'll take a long look at the extensive lore and history of giant birds in North America.

CHAPTER 5

The Mystery of the Balds

GIANT BIRD REPORTS CAN BE EXAMINED IN A CONTEXT of reports made across the North American continent. And, as we will see in a later chapter, such reports occur elsewhere in the world. Much support for extraordinary birds—both in specific stories and in persistent traditions—exists in the folklore of the United States and Canada. These traditions indicate that people have known about these birds for a long time.

Seventy-seven miles (124 kilometers) south of Odin, Illinois, lies Bald Knob Mountain, a 1,030-foot-high (314 meter) prominence topped by a giant white cross. Driving west from the community of Alto Pass toward Bald Knob, the winding road rises and drops beneath you, giving the impression that you are about to drive off a cliff at any moment. Eventually, one reaches the base of a grass-covered rise crowned by the immense white "People's Cross." The cross is 111 feet (34 meters) high and covered with white panels of porcelainized steel. Beneath it annual Easter services are held.

A walk to the top of Bald Knob on a clear day will give you a view of the country for more than 600 square miles (1554 square kilometers). The vista afforded by Bald Knob recalls similar bald knobs in the Eastern states of North Carolina and Georgia. Bare peaks in those states are associated in American Indian legend with man-eating giant birds.

The Indians said the peaks served as lookouts for early warning of the presence of the menacing birds. Could Bald Knob Mountain have served as an Indian lookout in prehistoric times? If so, there is no doubt about what those Indians were looking for because the Piasa—known also in popular discussions as The Bird That Devours Man—is famous in southern Illinois as an American Indian legend.

When Europeans first explored the Mississippi River in the 17th century, they noted two elaborately painted rock carvings on the side of the limestone bluff upon which Alton, Illinois, later grew up. The pictographs depicted monsters known as Piasas, winged creatures that once threatened the Indians. Close by, Piasa Creek cuts through the bluff and empties into the river.

Since the French Jesuit missionary Pere Marquette first noted these pictographs in 1673, their true appearance, size, and even the time of their destruction have been disputed. The apparent history of this native art has been assembled here from many sources, where disagreements were frequently encountered. [1]

Marquette came at a time when two pictographs were evident, though only the head remained for one of the two beasts. The cliff had fallen away where the body had been. He gave this description: "They are as large as a calf, with horns on the head like a deer, a fearful look, red eyes, bearded like a tiger, the face somewhat like a man's, the body covered with scales, and the tail so long

One conception of the Piasa drawing at Alton, Illinois Reprinted from Perry Armstrong, The Piasa, or, The Devil Among the Indians *(Morris, IL: 1887).*

THUNDERBIRDS

that it twice makes the turn of the body, passing over the head and down between the legs, and ending at last in a fish's tail. Green, red, and a kind of black, are the colors employed." [2]

Later travelers who came along, up to the year 1699, differed with Marquette, apparently because the appearance of the pictographs changed with the relative wetness and dryness of the seasons. They saw that the Piasa also had wings, and the reported height of them above the river varied with the rise and fall of the Mississippi. No reliable sketch of the pictographs has survived to this day, despite attempts in the 19th century to produce one.

Following the travel accounts of the 1600s, the pictographs seem to have escaped special notice for more than 100 years. On September 28, 1836, the Alton *Evening Telegraph* published an account of the Piasa legend among the Illini Indians. [3] This piece was probably written by John Russell of Bluffdale, who took a great interest in the Piasa legend. About this time, A.D. Jones visited the site and confirmed that, due to an Indian custom, the cliff face had been pockmarked by bullets fired at the monster by Indians passing on the river.

An artist, Henry Lewis, was sketching the Mississippi River scenery in this period for a panoramic painting of the river. A book later published in Germany contained his account of the "Piasa Rock" and a sketch of the pictograph site, but the editor of a recent English translation of the book noted that "whether or not Lewis saw the original is open to question." [4]

This spectacular native art apparently lasted until 1856 or 1857, when nearby quarrying by limemakers caused the rock to shatter and fall away, destroying the one complete carving. (The pictograph that was already disappearing in Marquette's time probably had disappeared prior to the 1800s.) Dates earlier and later (1846, 1870) are frequently given for its destruction. However, S.H. Russell, the son of John Russell, saw this art when he was a student at Shurtleff College in Alton in 1849. [5] Also, one Galus Paddock claimed to have seen it in 1852, when he was a boy of 15. [6] The figure definitely was gone when Francis Parkman passed the spot in 1867. [7]

The best description of the Piasa pictograph came from S.H. Russell, who had the following to say in an 1883 article:

> My recollection of it is of a picture cut into the surface of the rock to the depth of half an inch or more—had originally been painted red, black and blue, as portions of these colors were still adhering to the rock. The bird, or beast . . . had the head of a bear, directly facing the river below; the mouth was open, plainly showing large disproportioned teeth. On its head were the unmistakable horns of an elk. The upper portions of the horns were red, while the lower portions, together with the head, were black. The body was that of a fish confusedly colored with all three colors; it also showed distinctly the marks of scales, resembling in their order those of a fish. The wings were expanded to the right and left of the face, as if in the act of taking flight, extending probably from sixteen to eighteen feet [4.9 to 5.5 meters] from point to point. The legs were those of a bear, armed with the talons of an eagle. The tail was wrapped three times around the body, twice back of the wings, once forward, terminating in the shape of a spear head. The most prominent features were the wings and head, the latter being covered with a long beard or mane. [8]

Also vanished with the passage of time are the bones of the victims of the Piasa and the cave that held them. The September 28, 1836, issue of the Alton *Telegraph* contained this account of a visit to that cave by an unidentified writer, probably John Russell.

My curiosity was principally directed to the examination of a cave . . . in [sic] which the bird had carried its human victims. Preceded by an intelligent guide who carried a spade, I set out on my excursion. The cave was extremely difficult of access and at one point of our progress I stood at an elevation of more than one hundred and fifty feet on the face of the cliff, with barely room to sustain one foot. The unbroken wall towered above, while below was the river. After a long and perilous clambering, we reached the cave, which was about fifty feet [15 meters] above the surface of the river. By the aid of a long pole, placed on the projecting rock, and the upper end touching the mouth of the cave, we succeeded in entering it. Nothing could be more impressive than the view from the entrance of this cavern. The Mississippi was rolling in silent grandeur below us; high over our heads a single cedar hung its branches over the cliff, on the blasted top of which seated a bald eagle. No other sound or sign of life was near us. A Sabbath stillness rested upon the scene. Not a cloud was in the heavens; not a breath of air was stirring. The broad Mississippi lay before us, calm and smooth as a lake. The landscape presented the same wild aspect as it did before it had yet met the eye of the white man.

The roof of the cavern was vaulted, the top of which was hardly less than twenty-five feet [7.5 meters] in height. The shape of the cave was irregular, but so far as I could judge, the bottom would average twenty by thirty feet [6 by 9 meters]. The floor of this cave, throughout the whole extent, was a mass of human bones. Skulls and other human bones were mingled together in the utmost confusion. To what depth they descended I am unable to decide, but we dug to the depth of three or four feet in very quarter of the cavern, and still we found only bones . . . . [9]

The following are mere summaries of two lengthy legends regarding the Piasa. Father Louis Hennepin recorded a tradition among the Miami Indians of a feud between them and the Michegamies. Two monsters lived in a ravine between a Miami town at the site of Alton and a Michegamie town at the mouth of the Illinois River. At a time when these towns were engaged in battle, two Piasas appeared and carried off in their talons two Miami chieftains. As a result, the tide of battle turned in favor of the Miamis' enemies. The victors then engraved the images of the Piasas on the bluff. In later years, when they had regained their territory, the Miamis adopted the custom of firing arrows—and later bullets—at the rock images they could not erase. [10]

The Illini Indians had a separate tradition that told of a winged monster that made its home on the bluff. This powerful creature could carry off fully grown deer. It began to devour the Indians as well, causing a certain Illini chief, Ouatago, to seek help from the Great Spirit. Ouatago was thus inspired to execute a plan whereby he positioned himself at a high point along the river and waited for the Piasa. The monster appeared and was about to make the chief its victim when the poisoned arrows of 20 concealed Indians struck the Piasa, killing it. [11]

These traditions of the Piasa clearly indicate a longstanding knowledge of menacing giant birds in the heart of North America.

Two large caves along the Mississippi were credited in the 19th century as past homes of the dreaded Piasa, said to have contained numerous bones of victims of the beasts. The caves, like the pictographs, have vanished with time.

A widely printed—but clearly inadequate—depiction of the Piasa pictograph has been used to recreate the image on the modern river bluff in 1925, in 1934, and in 1961. So a reminder at least of the unparalleled Indian memorial may still be seen today at Alton—where descendants of the Piasa have been reported in recent decades.

The view from Bald Knob takes in much of southern Illinois and, in addition, may include the place of origin (and ultimate return destination) for the giant birds that make infrequent appearances in the news in Illinois. To the northwest, the twisting course of the Mississippi River can be glimpsed through the trees below Bald Knob. Further, to the west and a little to the south, a distinct hump is visible rising from the dark green of the forest. This hump is the St. Francois Mountains of southeastern Missouri, the beginning of the true Ozarks—and the most probable home for giant birds in the American Midwest. Somewhere in the Ozarks is the winter home of the Thunderbirds as they fly north in the spring and return south in the fall across Illinois. It can be said that the sightings of 1977 glimpsed two birds making their annual southerly flight and also a news sensation.

Those rumpled mountains of America's midlands, the Ozarks, have been poorly explored in any serious fashion for a history of animal stories. The folklore of the region has been taken down and characterized in the form of "windies" or colorful nonsense tales, such as can be found in Vance Randolph's *We Always Lie to Strangers*. This treatment, commonly applied by folklorists, categorizes all unusual stories as mere entertainment.

And so, when Randolph came to giant birds, he wrote in terms of "booger-owls" and the "giasticutus." The latter name occurs elsewhere in folklore and is most colorfully used in the context of a bunco scheme supposedly employed in the 19th century. Strangers in a small town would announce that they had captured the "terrible and feared gyascutus monster." They would proceed to charge admission to see the beast behind a curtain. The would-be spectators were then treated to cries of "The gyascutus is loose! Run for your life!" and the schemers would depart with their ill-gotten money. [12]

So to relate a story about something called the "giasticutus" is to brand it nonsense even before the story is told.

Randolph had this to say in 1951 about his "giasticutus" of Plains in Howell County, Missouri: "Only a few years ago there were men and women still alive who claimed to have seen the monster, which had a wingspread of about fifty feet [15.2 meters]. It was a bird of prey, like a prodigious chicken-hawk, with a great boat-like beak and a habit of carrying off full-grown cattle."

Enough time had passed that Randolph couldn't learn anything more definite about the bird, although he did come up with a few tidbits. From Greene County in Missouri he mentioned "a hawk 24 feet [7.3 meters] from tip to tip, which carried off a yearling calf," crediting a pamphlet by Floyd A. Yates.

In the Ozarks we hear the first—but not the last—of another creature, the giant owl. Randolph wrote that "tales of giant man-eating owls have been associated with Hemmed-In Holler, an almost inaccessible valley near Compton, Arkansas." After noting the limited size of known owls, he observed that "in many wild, isolated places one hears of enormous booger-owls with a wingspread of 10 or 12 feet [3 or 3.6 meters], so bold as to carry off lambs, calves, dogs, even children." [13]

From Bald Knob Mountain, the early Indian inhabitants of Illinois may have looked cautiously toward the Ozark Mountains for the creatures known in the Indian tradition as the Piasa and as the "giasticutus" in the white culture. The Indians may have scanned the skies in spring during the early morning and late evening hours for the silhouette of giant birds on the wing from those western mountains.

This speculation is encouraged by a tradition concerning the "balds" of the southern Appalachian Mountains. Certain Eastern peaks have long been a mystery to botanists and geologists, but are explained by the Cherokee Indians in a special way.

From Brasstown Bald, the highest point in the state of Georgia, one can look northward across North Carolina all the way to Clingman's Dome, the highest spot in Tennessee. [14] While Clingman's Dome is wooded all the way to its top, numerous lesser peaks from 2,000 to 6,000 feet (610 to 1829 meters) high—from Brasstown Bald northeast to Roan Mountain in Tennessee—are bare of trees. They've been so since the first white men arrived in the area. These "balds" are peculiar to the southern Appalachians and offer views of the surrounding mountains that otherwise would be impossible, due to what naturalist Ross Hutchins describes as the "dense, jungle-like walls of surrounding forest." [15]

The bare condition of so many and so widely scattered mountaintops has been the subject of many hypotheses. But no agreement has been found among foresters, geologists, and the like. Early theorists suggested the balds were caused by ice storms destroying all but the grass plants. Another thought that hot, dry winds from the southwest might have killed the trees. Fires and wind damage were put forth as possible causes as well. [16] Later ideas were that twig gall wasps were killing the timber or that a belt of olivine rock was causing thin soil through the area. [17]

Any hypothesis for the balds must explain the removal of trees from particular peaks, while many others were not affected. The plant that now dominates most of the balds is the mountain oat grass (*Danthonia compressa*), which is so dense that trees and bushes are unable to take hold. [18]

B. W. Wells, a botanist at North Carolina State College, suggested that Indians selected certain peaks as village sites and lookouts and that they burned off the original vegetation. He argued that the plant succession indicated artificial rather than natural fires. [19]

And, indeed, the Cherokee had their own explanation for the existence of the balds. According to them, the balds were created by the Cherokee ancestors to aid in defending their lives against giant predator birds. Stories of Tlanuwa, also known as the Great Mythic Hawk, were gathered from the Cherokee by James Mooney in the 19th century. And Herbert Ravenel Sass, in his book *Hear Me, My Chiefs!*, related Indian stories of this huge predatory bird, which was compared to a duck hawk or a peregrine falcon, only much greater in size. Its victims were large animals and the Indians themselves.

According to Sass, one of the last of the Tlanuwas was traced to its eyrie, or nesting place, by the use of lookouts on the mountain balds. The bird was thus seen to return to a cave on Whiteside Mountain, a spectacular crag 4,930 feet (1,503 meters) high that overlooks the Chattooga River in North Carolina. However, its eyrie proved to be unreachable for the Indians. The legend continued that the Tlanuwa was struck by lightning and fell from Whiteside Mountain into the valley below, where the Indians battled and killed the monster. [20]

James Mooney collected stories relating to another eyrie of the Tlanuwa, a cave above the Little Tennessee River below the mouth of Citico Creek in Blount County, Tennessee. The spot was known to the Cherokee as "Tlanuwai"—"the place of the Tlanuwa." Long ago, two Tlanuwas had made their nest in this cave, and they preyed on dogs and young Indian children. But the birds flew away forever after the Indians lowered a medicine man into the cave and he pushed four young birds from the nest into the river below. [21]

The Piasa of the Illinis and the Great Mythic Hawk of the Cherokees demonstrate that strong Indian traditions have existed and gain support from manmade landmarks on the North American continent. These traditions are variations of the famous Thunderbird, the legend that will be explored next.

CHAPTER 6

Sky Kings of the Past

THE IMAGE OF THE THUNDERBIRD ON A TOTEM POLE ranks as one of the most familiar symbols of American Indian cultures. No dictionary definition of Thunderbird seems complete without a totemic carving of the bird to illustrate and reinforce its mythological association with rain, lightning, and thunder. The symbolic Thunderbird is a giant bird that causes thunder by its wings and issues lightning from its eyes. And so large is this bird that, in the Pacific Northwest, it can carry men and whales away into the mountains. There is more to the life of the Thunderbird, however, as the following survey of American Indian lore reveals.

As shown in the previous chapter, giant birds of prey are known across the North American continent. In the eastern regions they're recorded among the Micmac of New Brunswick and Nova Scotia. Anthropologist Stansbury Hagar noted that the Culloo was a frightening winged creature that nested on a high cliff and fed moose and caribou to its young. A story was told of a hunter carried off by the Culloo to its nest. The man cleverly avoided being killed by the bird and joined two young birds in the nest. To escape his new home, he killed one of the young ones and used its wings to glide to safety. [1]

This story in general outline is identical to a Cherokee story collected by James Mooney about "the hunter and the Tlanuwa." There the hunter escaped from a cave nest by strapping himself to a young Tlanuwa and so being carried safely to the ground. [2] This kind of similarity in stories has caused students of Thunderbird lore to regard the tales as lacking in substance, as being shared among or borrowed from other Indian groups. Another view of them would be that, while perhaps lacking literal truth in many cases, they served as a means to pass on from generation to generation

A Haida Indian carving of a Thunderbird. Drawn by the author after a photograph in Veronica Irons, The World's Mythology in Color *(London: Hamlyn, 1947)*

information about genuine giant birds that were part of the American Indians' environment. These birds could actually threaten the Indians. The narratives were given sustained life by genuine cases of encounters between hunters and Thunderbirds.

THUNDERBIRDS

Physical evidence to support a story has been reported with another tradition from New Brunswick. A giant bird called Cullona was known to the Saint John River Indians (who are widely identified as the Malecite Indians, though the name "Malecite" was a term of reproach applied to them by the Micmac [3]). Another collector of folklore, Edward Jack, recorded information about the Cullona from a note by James Hannay published in the *Telegraph Press* of St. John, New Brunswick, in 1875. This bird nested on high rocks or mountains and once carried off a boy of eight or ten years. But two young birds in the nest were already well fed and refused to eat this new victim, so the Cullona returned the boy to where he was captured. Hannay noted that, when passing by a certain rocky mountain in a canoe, the Indians told him, "There is the nest of the great bird that carried away the boy." And Hannay found "a great number of sticks, put together like a nest, on the top of the mountain." Another time, they pointed out a bird, saying it was a smaller bird of the same kind. Hannay described the bird they indicated as "a large and speckled one, like an eagle, though somewhat larger." [4] Charles Leland noted the Culloo as a fierce predatory bird in Micmac and Passamaquoddy tales. [5]

In Labrador, among the Montagnais-Naskapi, the Indians knew "Met'co the Eagle Abductor" that snatched a boy from a lakeshore and flew off as others watched helplessly. At a nest "on the great rocks," this boy too was not eaten. He stayed there a full summer before grasping the leg of the eagle as it left the nest, and he reached the ground and returned home. [6]

A giant bird has a part in the Indian legends of Massachusetts. The legendary character Maushope tracked this bird, as noted by A. Hyatt Verrill: "At that time there was a giant bird who raided the Indians' villages and carried off the children, and Maushope, pursuing the great bird, waded across to Nantucket where he found the bones of the missing children piled in a mound beneath a big tree." [7]

In the West, powerful birds other than the Thunderbird

were also known. The Navaho in the Southwest knew of Tse'na'hale, which was "something like an eagle in form." A legend associated with Winged Rock told of its carrying a warrior to a ledge there. [8] A monster bird with feathers like knives, Achiyalabopa, was known to the Pueblo Indians. [9]

In northeastern New Mexico, the volcanic peak of Capulin Mountain has a Thunderbird legend associated with it. One origin for the name of the mountain is that choke cherries (*capulin* in Spanish) grow there. Another tells a story about an Indian named Capulin. He saw his brother kill a Thunderbird, the guardian of the volcano. The volcanic crater became active, threatening to destroy the Indians. Capulin threw himself into the mouth of the volcano, causing it to subside, and he saved his people. [10]

The Shoshoni, or Snake, Indians of the Great Basin feared the giant bird Nunyenunc, which carried off men, but wasn't associated with thunder. [11] This appears to be the same menace identified only as the "Behemoth Bannock Bird" by Elmer Sparks writing in *Frontier Times* for Winter 1960. Sparks writes that several Great Basin tribes—the Shoshoni, Bannocks, Paiutes, and Gosiute—had related stories of a bird five times the size of an eagle. It carried away deer, antelope, and mountain sheep to be devoured. Abner Blackburn, who traveled eastward through Utah in 1847, reportedly told his relatives about such birds. [12]

From the Great Lakes, through the Great Plains, across the Columbia Plateau, and along the Northwest Coast, knowledge of the Thunderbird proper has been recorded in abundance. Campbell Grant notes in *Rock Art of the American Indian* its appearance in rock art in these areas and in the Southwest. The bird always is shown with its head to one side and its wings spread wide. The Thunderbird motif has been expressed in wood, fabric, and the earth of effigy mounds. It has served as a clan symbol, as with the Eagle Clan of the Hopi and the Thunderbird Clan of the Winnebago. [13]

There is no doubt that the Piasa of the Illini was identical to the Thunderbird, because A.F. Chamberlain, in his discussion of the latter belief among the Algonkians, gives the following information: "The Thunderbird is called piyesis—i.e., 'bird'—identical with Ojebway binesi, Mississagua pinesi, Illinois pineusen, Ottawa pinasi, evidently a common Algonkian word for 'bird.'" [14]

These avian masters of storms left their mark on the land around the Great Lakes in place names. The high rocks near Thunder Bay at Alpena, Michigan, were the home of the Thunderbirds, according to the Potawatomi Indians. [15] Thunder Bay, Ontario, took its name from a translation of "Animike Wekwed," or "Thunder Bird Bay." Thunder Lake, Wisconsin, was also named for the legendary bird. [16]

A roost of the bird was often associated with these places; a nest containing young Thunderbirds was said to have been found at Thunder Bay, Michigan. [17] The Ojibwe, or Chippewa, told George Laidlaw that "a long time ago" in Ontario, their people made repeated visits to a nest with two young birds located on an escarpment in the Blue Mountains south of Nottawasaga Bay. [18] Mt. Mckay, a butte with sheer cliffs west of Thunder Bay, Ontario, was identified by the Ojibwe as a home of the Thunderbirds. [19]

In *Wisconsin Indian Place-Name Legends*, Dorothy M. Brown recorded that the Potawatomi identified Thunder Mountain in Marinette County for the Chequah, one of the giant birds believed to explain thunder. This hill was known to these Indians as a frequent nesting site of Thunderbirds. [20] Brown also recorded an Ojibwe legend telling of the Chenemeke, a mighty but invisible Thunderbird. The Okibwe identified a certain place as the "forest destroyed by the great Thunderbird." [21]

An example of a generic tale of a hunter carried away by a giant bird is this one recorded in 1915 among the Menominee Indians of Wisconsin:

> Once upon a time an Indian was out hunting
> when he heard a great roaring or rushing sound
> in the air above him. He looked up and all

around but could see nothing. At last he gave up
trying to see the maker of the disturbance, but no
sooner had he turned his back, than something
dropped out of the sky and seized him. It was a
monstrous bird, and it began to soar away with
him in its talons. Frightened terribly, he pretend-
ed to be dead for fear the bird would drop him.
As they rose in the air the earth began to recede
from his sight until it took upon itself the size and
appearance of a little green apple. At last, the bird
lit upon a great rock that seemed to be floating
way up in the sky among the clouds . . . .

After the bird had laid him down, it flew away. Then:

. . . he came across a great nest, in which he found
two young birds of great size, almost old enough
to fly. . . . He destroyed them with his spear. In
their nest he found the bones of many dead
animals . . . . Some of them he recognized as
being those of the great horned snakes . . . . He
skinned out the body of one of the nestlings leaving its head and wings.

Using the wings he leaped from the rock and drifted to a
safe landing near his old hunting grounds. [22]

Thunder's Nest (*Wakiyan Hurpi* to the Dakota Indians),
Thunderbird's Track (*Wakiyan Oye*), and Thunderbird's Track's
Brother are sites in the vicinity of eastern South Dakota. In 1883, the
Sisseton and Wahpeton Indians told Theodore H. Lewis about a
Thunderbird having built a nest of sticks and brush on a mound 10
miles (16 kilometers) northwest from the outlet of Lake Traverse.
(This location can still be found on modern topographic maps
marked as "Devil's Nest," just over the border in North Dakota.) A

great flood caused the bird to depart the area, and Wakiyan Oye was where the bird left its impression before departing. Lewis traced petroglyphs (rock carvings) at that site and its "brother" nearby, but these glyphs were dissimilar to each other, even unlike bird tracks, and were, he thought, already very old. [23]

The Ojibwe, the Dakota, and the Menomini (in Wisconsin) all had stories of the Thunderbird. [24] Anthropologist Stanley Vestal wrote that his Dakota Indian friends had seen the birds. A Hunkpapa Dakota, Gray Whirlwind, had seen four of them sitting on a high bluff. Another said he had once captured such an unusual bird. [25]

The legend was known to the Cheyenne, Arapaho, Kiowa, and Comanche. In the southern Plains the Comanche associated the landing of the Thunderbird (ba'a') with a spot of earth burned in the shape of a bird on the upper Red River. [26]

Much has been preserved of the Blackfoot Indians' knowledge of large birds, due to the work done 50 years ago by Claude Schaeffer of the Museum of the Plains Indians in Browning, Montana. [27] The Blackfoot were three tribes—the Piegan (Pikuni), the Blood (Kainteh), and the North Blackfoot (Siksika)—who once occupied the northern plains east of the Rocky Mountains, from the North Saskatchewan River in Alberta to the Yellowstone River in Montana. [28] Schaeffer began his paper on the subject with this summary: "Elderly Blackfoot Indians, in recounting faunal lore of a now vanished past, sometimes refer to an immense bird, which visited the eastern foothills and adjacent plains of the Montana-Alberta region. Nearly a half century has elapsed, at least, since it was last sighted in this region."

He first learned of such a bird when, after recording Indian names for the golden eagle, the bald eagle, and the turkey vulture, his informants insisted there was another large raptor they called "Omaxsapitau" or "big pitau" ("pitau" was their name for the golden eagle). Schaeffer thought that this bird could only have been the California condor and argued for this interpretation in his paper. He talked with the eldest Indians in Browning, who were mostly Piegan, and he learned also of some traditions of Blood origin. They told him of events dating from the mid 19th century into the early years of the 20th century. The Indians gave accounts of seeing the Omaxsapitau.

In the 1860s, the parents of Dog Takes a Gun saw one near Calgary. In the same decade, Piegan warriors led by Heavy Runner took the sight of one as a bad omen, and therefore turned back from a raid on the Crow Indians.

A surviving Piegan, Rides at the Door, had seen one on a raid to the south. In 1879, the daughter of Red Paint, Mary Jane, and her white husband (Pfemster or Pheminster) observed four extraordinary birds at Chief Mountain. This peak is now included in Glacier National Park in northwestern Montana. They thought two of the birds were just learning to fly, watched by the larger parents that had a nest on the mountain that summer.

In 1897 Big Crow and his wife were returning to their home in the southern part of the Blackfoot Reservation when they spied a dark object from far off. When nearer they realized it was "an immense, dark-colored bird, with a feathered ruff and a bald head." It flew away to the mountains.

Piegan Indians learned around 1907–08 in a letter from Gros Ventre Indians that a large bird had been seen around Montana's Fort Belknap Reservation.

The most recent appearance of this "big eagle" that Schaeffer heard of was around 1908, when George Bull Child and others saw two or three of them on the Blackfoot Reservation.

The most extraordinary experiences happened to White Bear, a Cree who married into the Blood tribe and lived with them as a conjurer and eagle trapper. He died in 1905 at about the age of 83. His grandson, Harry Under Mouse, related the following events about White Bear. Around 1850, White Bear was trapping eagles in the area south of present-day Edmonton. The feathers of the golden eagle were valued for ceremonial uses. To capture the birds, a trapper concealed himself in a shallow pit, which was lightly camouflaged and baited with a stuffed animal. Instead of the expected eagle, which a skilled trapper could seize by the legs and kill, a much larger and more formidable bird, an Omaxsapitau, circled and landed at White Bear's trap. He took the stick he kept to scare off bald eagles and used it to startle the bird and it left.

White Bear's next experience, related at length and in detail by his grandson, involved his being carried off by one of these powerful birds in the classic style of "the hunter and the Culloo/Tlanuwa/Thunderbird." One winter when food was scarce, the Blood tribe was camped near the present site of Edmonton. Repeatedly, and mysteriously, hunters would lose one of their number from small hunting parties that were desperately seeking food.

White Bear was one of a party of four who traveled a long distance and then built a shelter near Devil's Head Mountain, which lies to the northeast of the site of Banf. These men scattered to hunt in different directions. When White Bear did not rejoin the other three, they traced his footprints in the snow to a point where they simply ended. They found his bow close by. The hunters returned home and were mourning White Bear's death when he appeared at the lodge of his wife and parents very much alive. He told them how he had disappeared—and as evidence he produced two feathers nearly as long as a man's arm.

As White Bear explained, he had slain a deer and fixed the butchered meat in a pack. Using his bow as a cane, he walked toward the hunters' shelter hunched over with the pack on his back. He saw the shadow of a bird just before it grasped his pack and lifted him off his feet. With his eyes closed in fear, he waited until he felt himself touch earth again. He found himself in a large nest containing the bones of deer and bison calves. To his horror, he saw human bones as well, almost certainly the earthly remains of the missing hunters.

The giant bird that transported him was close by, and two young birds were in the nest. To escape the nest, which was high on a cliff, he attracted the young ones with chunks of meat and then grasped their legs. Tumbling out of the nest, the birds' wings checked his drop to earth enough to save him. He pulled the longest feathers from their tails as trophies and then returned to this people.

Schaeffer noted the similarity to the Roc legend, as anthropologists label all such stories, and chose to regard this testimony as mere insubstantial folklore because it didn't suit his argument that the condor was the Omaxsapitau. But here we have a record of an individual who plausibly possessed the skills necessary to save himself from a fate that was often fatal to others. As an eagle trapper, he was experienced in grasping the legs of raptors and didn't hesitate to do so when it was necessary to gain his freedom. Franz Boas discussed the many Thunderbird legends in his collection of Kutenai tales made to the west of the Blackfoot. [29]

Also from the region of the Columbia Plateau, word of giant birds came to this writer by way of Rene Dahinden, pursuer of the legendary Sasquatch and co-author with Don Hunter of the book *Sasquatch*. According to Dahinden, the modern-day Yakima Indians in Washington told Bigfoot hunter Roger Patterson stories of giant birds. [30] The Kathlamet Indians on the lower Columbia River knew the Thunderbird as "an abductor of maidens," according to writer Dale Ott. [31]

In California the Southern Miwok Indians along the Merced River had stories telling of a gigantic bird called *Yel'-lo-kin*. C. Hart Merriam recorded this characterization of it: "Yel'-lo-kin was a giant bird—the biggest bird in the world. He was in the habit of carrying off children—boys and girls up to fourteen or fifteen years of age. He took them by the top of the head and carried them up through the hole in the middle of the sky to his home on top of the sky, where he killed and ate them." [32]

The creature called the Thunderbird has been known in Mexico and, most importantly, anthropologists and naturalists found it among the Indians on the western coast of North America, from the mouth of the Columbia River all the way to Prince William Sound in Alaska. [33] The Chinook and Chehalis near Gray's Harbor called it Hahness. [34] The Olympic Peninsula of

Washington is certainly the hub of western Thunderbird lore. And what better home for wonders could there be than the glacier-capped Olympic Mountains? Wet Pacific winds blow over the peninsula, creating the wettest climate in the contiguous United States. Temperate rainforests fill valleys on the western side, while the northeastern side of the peninsula stays relatively dry.

On the western side, the Quinault, Hoh, Quilleute, Makah, and Klallam Indians all knew the Thunderbird and told anthropologists about it. Furthermore, the stories of birds carrying off whales, recorded among the Hoh and Quilleute, rang all too true to the people in this region. [35] The Twana Indians, who were in control of the Hood Canal region to the end of the 1850s, said their hunters sometimes found nests of the Thunderbirds in the mountains—and they also found whale bones there too, bones that they considered sacred. [36] The Quinault even had a story of a whale found thrashing about on a mountain with its dorsal fin missing. After it died, they took its fat and meat. Long after that, its bones were still seen covered with moss. [37]

A Thunderbird with a whale. This image was painted on a Nootka Indian drum in British Columbia. Drawn by the author from a photograph in Edward A. Armstrong, The Life and Lore of the Bird *(NY: Crown, 1975).*

To the north, on Vancouver Island, a mountain behind Clayoquot was known to the Makahs as a home of the Thunderbird. Whale bones littered the shore of a lake there. [38] The Thunderbird was sacred to the Nootka of Vancouver Island. It was known as Kwunusela to the Kwakiutl. [39] The Bella Coola knew it as Alkuntam. [40] It was Oolala to the Haidah of the Queen Charlotte Islands, where James Swan claimed that it preyed on whales and Indians, similar to the Theukloots or Dukwally of the Makahs. [41]

The menace of Thunderbirds that once seems to have hung over the Pacific coast is described in these paragraphs. The beliefs were taken down by James Swanton a century ago among the Tlingit Indians of Alaska. After noting the associations with rain, thunder, and lightning, he wrote:

> The thunder bird [sic] keeps on thundering and the sky continues cloudy until the bird catches a whale. Then it carries the whale up into the mountains, where bones of whales caught in the summer may often be seen. A hunter from Daxe't was once overtaken by a thunderstorm and was blinded by a great flash. When he finally looked up he saw a big thunder bird astride of a mountain. It had the general appearance of an eagle. Another time some Sitka people out in a choppy place in the ocean heard thundering going on in a certain direction and, repairing to that point next day, found a whale lodged in the trees with claw marks on it. A Russian vessel was almost carried away by one of these birds because the sailors had made fun of it. [42]

William H. Dall also recorded the Tlingit knowledge of this "myth" in the Alaskan panhandle, including the story of the bird Kunna-kat-eth at home on Mount Edgecumbe, opposite Sitka. [43]

The Tlingit also had stories of Thunderbird sightings, finding feathers and seeing whale bones in a glacier near Katalla, Alaska. [44]

Knowledge of Thunderbirds extended to the Innuit, or Eskimos, as well. Henry Rink, in his collection of Eskimo traditions, included only that they knew of Serdlernaks, which were "fabulous birds." [45] But naturalist William H. Dall was surprised by his colleague Edward W. Nelson, when Nelson produced a carved image of the Thunderbird from the Diomede Islands in the Bering Strait. [46]

Nelson also recorded an Eskimo story of the "last of the Thunderbirds (Mu-Tugh-O-Wik)" from along the lower Yukon River. Long ago, many giant eagles lived in the mountains, but they declined in numbers until only one pair remained nesting on a mountain near Sabotnisky. (In 1899, Sabotnisky was an Eskimo village on the right bank of the Yukon River, near present-day Fortuna Ledge, Alaska. [47])

The birds preyed on reindeer and helpless Eskimos, who were carried off to be eaten. The birds sealed their doom when, one summer day, they made off with the wife of a young hunter. To avenge her death, he took his bow and war arrows and climbed to the nest, where he dispatched the young eagles. He hid nearby and greeted the returning parents with arrows as well. Pierced but still able to fly, the giants flew off to the north and were gone for good. Nelson added this footnote to the story: "The truth of this tale is implicitly believed by the Eskimo on the lower Yukon. They point out the crater of an old volcano as the nest of the giant eagles, and say that the ribs of old canoes and curiously colored stones carried there by the bird may still be seen about the rim of the nest. This is one of the various legends of the giant eagles or thunderbirds that are familiar to the Eskimo of the Yukon and to those of Bering Strait and Kotzebue Sound." [48]

This survey of the Thunderbird Indian legends ends at Kotzebue Sound, on the northwest corner of Alaska. The next chapter begins an examination of the pioneer and modern accounts of giant birds. They begin at this same Kotzebue Sound, where descendants of those mighty Thunderbirds might still be seen today.

CHAPTER 7

Thunderbirds West

DESPITE THE EXISTENCE OF THE THUNDERBIRD LEGEND and its promotion by Jack Pearl, the notion of living giant birds has not been widely known or accepted in North America. Only the state of Pennsylvania—as we will explore in chapter 9—has a giant bird tradition that encouraged the reporting of monster birds. Nevertheless, a history of encounters, mainly brief ones, exists in many states. Some detailed accounts of extraordinary events—as already seen in Illinois—are also on record. From Alaska to California, across the Southern states, and up the Appalachian Mountains to Canada, odd events have come to light from the shadows of the bird world. We will begin with the western half of North America.

From Alaskan towns near Kotzebue Sound, according to *Alaska* magazine, reports were made in 1970 and 1972 of "super birds" in the mountains. Mr. and Mrs. Evelyn Barr at Noorvik reported one that looked bigger than a Twin Otter airplane; the Otter Floatplane De Havilland has a span of 58 feet (17.7 meters). The Barrs thought it was looking for caribou to eat. Another giant bird was reported near Selawik and north of Kivalina in 1970. [1] As related earlier in chapter 1, gigantic birds have been making news in Alaska as recently as October 2002.

In the Canadian Rockies, the Tower of Babel is a peak 7,592 feet (2,314 meters) high and located about 6 miles (9.6 kilometers) southeast of Lake Louise in Alberta. It was the site of the following report given by Dan McCowan in his *Animals of the Canadian Rockies*. "In early July of 1925 two visitors to Consolation Valley saw an eagle flying at a considerable height. As it neared the Tower of Babel, an immense buttress of rock, it came much lower and they observed that the big brown bird carried an animal of considerable size in its talons." Loud yells of the observers caused the bird to drop what they found to be a fawn of a mule deer. A park warden at Lake Louise, Harold Fuller, weighed the fawn at nearly 15 pounds (6.8 kilograms). [2]

A bird of prey lifting a weight exceeding a few pounds is extraordinary. Such reports have been disputed among naturalists because of doubts that known birds have such lifting ability. An alternative possibility, not usually considered, is that extraordinary birds not recognized by ornithologists are responsible for the unusual reports.

On February 7, 1954, just south of the Olympic Peninsula at Hillsboro, Oregon, west of Portland, Gladie M. Bills saw to her wonder six giant birds flapping their wings. Even at a great height they looked the size of airplanes. She watched them for about five minutes, and her daughter, age 17, also saw them. The birds circled and dived on the sunny day with high, thin clouds. Gladie Bills wrote to *Fate* magazine about her observations. The letters column of this popular magazine has served since 1948 as a forum for people to tell their unusual experiences. [3] After all, anyone who sees such things as Thunderbirds has few places to go to tell their story.

Ray Crowe has preserved one sighting of a giant bird in his periodical devoted to modern stories of unusual animals, *The Track Record*. He told of an encounter in the summer of 1978, when Jessie Ross saw something that looked to him like "a prehistoric eagle" sitting on a large rock east of Arco, Idaho. As Ross approached, it tried to fly off, but it had difficulty getting airborne. It took "lumbering steps," but eventually got off the ground and caught the warm summer thermals. It disappeared to the north. Ross said that it was 5 feet (1.5 meters) tall when standing and was as black as coal. Its head was a bright orange and it had a hook at the end of its beak. When it got in the air, he could see a wingspan of about 20 to 22 feet (6 to 6.6 meters). [4]

Large birds have always been seen in the skies of California. The state has been the home of the last known surviving North American condors in the wild. Condors normally can reach a wingspan of 9 to 11 feet (2.7 to 3.2 meters). The greatest span ever recorded in a captured specimen was 11 feet, 4 inches (3.4 meters), in 1908. Condor specialists are forced to consider the possibility that larger birds once existed because they were described in the 1800s. According to San Francisco's *Daily Alta California*, a newspaper of the 1850s, a bird with a 14-foot (4.2-meter) span made off with a 9-pound (4 kilogram) rabbit. James Clyman was an early and trustworthy observer, according to Dick Smith in his book *Condor Journal*, and Clyman claimed to have seen birds that big at different times. [5]

But even larger specimens of known condors would not fly off with even a rabbit because these birds are carrion feeders. In fact, they don't carry food any distance with their weak feet. And what else but Thunderbirds could be responsible for the many stories writer Dale Ott has heard that tell of the truly harmless condors supposedly snatching children and young wildlife? [6]

A collection of horrific monster accounts placed at and near Elizabeth Lake in southern California was written some 60 years ago by Horace Bell. [7] He presented his primary source as an historical record, but it was truly a collection of local folklore. [8] Among the monster stories was a tale of disappearing horses and cattle in 1883, when ranch hands were awakened one night by noises from a horse corral. They discovered ten horses gone and saw an "incredible griffon" flying off into the night.

The Oakland *Tribune* reported a modern sighting. In early October 1975, a resident of Walnut Creek, California, looked behind his house to see a huge bird dwarfing a large eucalyptus tree. Lloyd King described the thing as more than 5 feet (1.5 meters) in height with "a head like a vulture." Its wings were gray. King summoned his children and neighbors to watch as well. After five minutes, the bird glided away effortlessly, showing a wingspan of approximately 15 feet (4.6 meters). Vincent Minelli said he, his wife, and neighbors all saw a creature the same size as King's sitting on the roof of a building behind the International Institute of Eastbay. He heard something like an owl. [9]

More than 100 years earlier, at Winnemucca Lake in western Nevada, a farmer, his family, and neighbors were treated to a similar spectacle. Resting on the barn was something that looked to be 7 feet (2.1 meters) long from its beak to its tail. Wings 12 feet (3.6 meters) across were displayed when it flew, according to the St. Catherines (Ontario) *Evening Journal* of September 20, 1871. [10]

In the wide-open spaces of the American West, appearances of bird wonders tend to be brief. On July 18, 1966 a big bird had Salt Lake City residents eager for a look. One witness, C.L. Fairbanks, compared its size to a Piper Cub airplane. It circled the area and flew off to the east, according to the *Deseret News*. [11]

In the summer of 1970, Jesus Martinez of Donna, Texas, was driving between Donna and Weslaco at night. During his trip he spied a bird "as long as an automobile." Its wings stretched the width of road, 16 feet (4.9 meters). This bird had the bill and head of an eagle and looked "brownish" with a V-shaped tail. [12]

Merle Rose of Amarillo, Texas, did not have to leave home to see his giant bird in the summer of 1975. It perched on his house and made sounds like "whoo, whoo, whoo." When it took off, its flapping wings "sucked a whole bush from the ground" in front of him. [13]

Another "huge bird" made headlines in eastern Texas in 1976. At the time, this writer appealed to newspapers in that area but couldn't get a single response on the subject. Therefore, we're indebted to fortean researchers such as Tom Adams, Tim Church, and David Fideler who circulated news stories from the Palestine (Texas) *Herald Press*. [14]

As the story goes, from December 6 to 22 a large bird (presumably the same one) was seen by different people around Bethel and Montalba. The most detailed encounter took place around 2:00 p.m. on December 8, when John S. Carroll Jr., a prominent swine breeder, came upon a bird standing in his pond. From a distance of less than 150 feet (45.7 meters), he observed the following features:

- A height of 8 feet (2.4 meters)
- Wingspread of 10 to 12 feet (3 to 3.6 meters)
- Bluish steel-gray feathers
- A breast with a golden tinge
- A brownish-gray beak 12 inches (30 cm) long
- Two eyes that bugged out, 6 inches (15 cm) apart
- A neck 3 feet (90 cm) long

The bird took off with apparent difficulty, circled, and landed in a distant hardwood tree on a hill to the northwest of Carroll. He fetched his deer rifle and scope from his pickup truck. Taking careful aim, he fired at the bird causing it to drop out of sight. Hurrying to the tree, only a bloody and broken feather no more than 3 inches (76 mm) long was found.

A brief item emerged from Possum Kingdom Dam near Ranger, Texas, at the end of 1944, when two people observed a "gigantic bird" wading and taking off. [15]

One of the most extraordinary experiences with giant birds occurred to Gladwell Richardson (1903-1980), the son of a rancher and trader who grew up in Oklahoma. He attended the Oklahoma Mechanical and Technical College (which became Oklahoma State University), and became a prolific author on Western themes. He wrote reminiscences of his boyhood under the name "Maurice Kildare." A lengthy account of those years appeared in *True Frontier* magazine of October 1972. [16]

Richardson's father had run a ranch in the Red Hills of Oklahoma's Coal County. When his family arrived at the ranch, a community of people was already living on a portion of the land. They'd been living there as long as anyone could remember, apparently a settlement of the first white people to enter the area, probably two centuries earlier. They kept to themselves, and married mostly within their own group of several families. Richardson compared their lives to the people depicted in the Dogpatch cartoon strip. They had made no legal claims on the land. They had simply always lived there. Rather than try to run them off, Richardson's father was clever enough to strike a bargain with them. For the cost of a few cattle to help feed their families each year, they became the rancher's allies in protecting his ranch and stock from cattle rustlers. This proved to be a wise bargain.

Richardson grew up in the company of these people, and he knew them well and learned their stories. As a young man, he was shown the remains of a giant bird that had been killed years before. As they explained the story, for many months in the mid 19th century, before the Civil War, an immense bird terrorized this pioneer community. Many people encountered a bird that stood taller than a man. Each wing was at least 8 feet (2.4 meters) long. Its color was gray, and it gave off a suffocating odor. The bird was a threat to calves, colts, dogs, deer, and children when it made its appearances every month or two.

Two men survived lengthy battles on the ground with the monster bird. Its tenacity in this struggle is characteristic of birds, i.e., once they attack, they persist. Richardson confirmed the accounts of the bird with witnesses. The bird was finally shot by a hunter who killed it as it swooped over some deer. When still a boy, Richardson was shown the burial site of the bird. He helped to dig up the rotten remains of the feathers and bones of the beast.

When he had grown up, Richardson left the area and didn't return for many years. Upon his return to the Red Hills, he found the settlers had entirely disappeared. Only a few wooden tombstones remained to show that they had ever been there.

CHAPTER 8

Thunderbirds East

THESE GIANT BIRDS HAVE CAUSED AWE AND DISBELIEF due to their extraordinary physical appearance and the locations of where they have been observed in flight. A greater volume of historical reports comes from the Midwest and Eastern regions of North America than in the West. One obvious reason is the denser human population in the East and Midwest, although other reasons will be discussed in chapter 10, where the habits of the birds will be described.

As already explained, Wisconsin and Illinois have been the scene of Thunderbird appearances as recently as 1977 and 1988. But in Illinois in 1968, an eyewitness spotted the bird but waited 26 years to make it known. The witness, artist David St. Albans of Albuquerque, New Mexico, wrote to the magazine *World Explorer* in 1994 to tell of his experience as a young man in northern Illinois. In July 1968, he was visiting his father in Keeneyville, Illinois. After mowing his father's lawn, he spied a large bird approaching from the west. It had the shape of a hawk and flapped its wings slowly. It flew past him, giving him a good look at it: "As it came closer it appeared not as an eagle but exactly as the Lawndale witnesses described their avian raptor. It appeared to be an immense condor, very much like those living in California and the Andes. It was that big, perhaps bigger. Its head was indeed naked and pink. The rest of the body [was] dull black but with a tuft of white feathers at the base of the neck. The neck itself was indeed at least a foot long!"

St. Albans' bird had a long yellowish-orange beak. At the front of the beak was a "vicious" hook. What St. Albans took to be interlocking "teeth" on the beak probably indicated a serrated bill, which would be an asset to a creature that takes large and live prey. [1]

St. Albans said he nearly froze with fear, which is understandable when one considers the formidable eating-machine he described. The bird flew low past him and disappeared to the east.

As told in chapter 4, pigs and lambs were lost to "eagles" in 1868 in Tippah County in Mississippi, and then even a young boy died after being lifted high in the air by a bird.

Perhaps a descendant of that formidable "eagle" made an appearance 110 miles (177 kilometers) to the northeast of Tippah County in 1975. In Tennessee, Eddy Reese of Lewisburg was returning home from Alabama on Interstate Highway 65. As his car topped a hill where the road cut through a mountain, a giant bird swooped over his car. Its wings extended over both lanes of the highway. The creature's coloration was dark. Reese had the feeling that the bird was attacking, but then it disappeared and wasn't seen again. This information was gathered by Duncan Murphy, another persistent fortean researcher. [2]

The proximity of a giant bird to a moving vehicle and the impression of a menacing attack have been reported elsewhere. The likely explanation for this behavior isn't that the bird is attacking, but that it's using the draft of the moving vehicle to assist it in getting airborne. The birds seem to rely on soaring flight and exploit air currents however they can.

The earliest giant bird report from Illinois dates from 1868. Credit for revealing this item goes to Benoit Crevier of Montreal, Quebec, who has provided me with a copy of a news report from the Atlanta (Georgia) *Constitution* for September 18, 1868. This paper reprinted an item from the Cairo (Illinois) *Democrat* titled "A Singular Bird Killed in Kentucky" concerning a bird killed across the Ohio River from Mound City. Here is the complete news report.

> James Henry, of Mound City, Illinois, shot a new
> and comparatively unknown bird, on the
> Kentucky shore opposite that city, which is thus
> described by the Cairo *Democrat*:

It is larger than the ostrich, and weighs 104 pounds [47 kilograms]. The body of this wonderful bird is covered with snow white down and its head is of a fiery red. The wings, of deep black, measure 15 feet [4.6 meters] from tip to tip, and the bill, of a yellow color, 24 inches [61 cm]. Its legs are slender and sinewy, pea green in color, and measure 48 inches [122 cm] in length. One of the feet resembles that of a duck, and the other that of a turkey. Mr. Henry shot it at a distance of one hundred yards [90 meters], from the topmost branch of a dead tree, where it was perched, preying upon a full-sized sheep that it had carried from the ground. This strange species of bird, which is said to have existed extensively during the days of the mastodon, is almost entirely extinct—the last one having been seen in the State of New York during the year 1812. Potter has it on exhibition in his office at Mound City. Its flight across the town and river was witnessed by hundreds of citizens. [3]

The size and predatory behavior of the bird suggest it to be the Thunderbird. The different feet ascribed to it may be an attempt to describe the appearance of a damaged bird.

In addition to all the reports given so far for Illinois, the state has seen modern reports in 1968 around Galesburg. Grant and Wilma Callison reported observing three birds on May 10, 1968. They estimated the wingspans to be 15 to 20 feet (4.6 to 6 meters). Grant Callison's brother and his wife also saw the birds from a different location. In October 1968, another bird of similar size was observed over Galesburg. [4]

The state of Florida may have been the scene of bird visits, but very little has been put on the record. Along the Tamiami Trail in the south huge wings and "a kind of rushing sound" were the memorable features of a bird seen during the winter of 1960-61. Curtis Fuller, the editor of *Fate* magazine, passed this along in his regular column, "I See by the Papers," in May 1961. He cited the Miami *Herald* as the story's source. One woman told the paper she had seen a bird like a vulture with a wingspread she guessed to be over 50 feet (15.2 meters). [5]

The first of Kentucky's contributions to unusual bird files came in 1870. The following news dispatch appeared in the St. Paul (Minnesota) *Press* for January 11, 1870 under the headline "Sinbad's Roc."

CAPTURE OF WONDERFUL SEVEN-FOOT BIRD IN LINCOLN COUNTY

From the Stanford (Ky.) Dispatch

Mr. James Pepples, living two and half miles from Stanford, on the Dudderar's mill road, is surrounded by a party of neighboring boys, who are fond of the sport of night hunting. Over a week ago these were engaged in their favorite pastime, and, while absorbed in the excitement of a fox chase, were suddenly startled by what they called an unearthly scream from some of the tree tops. Some declared it was a panther, some a cata-mount, and others believed the voice that of a female in distress. They agreed to approach as near the spot from whence the screams came as possible, and took up the line of march toward the place.

At each step the screams were repeated, to the amazement of the boys, and, if truth must be told, there was a perceptible terror in each one's voice, and daylight would have exhibited very pale faces. Guided still nearer by the strange noise, they directly heard the clink of chains, irons and padlocks. This was too much for the youthful temerity to endure. They were brave boys, but demoniac yells from the tree tops, accompanied by rattling music of the devil at the dreary hour of midnight, when ghosts, hobgoblins, and blue devils stalk abroad, were fraught with too much impending danger to be relished even by stouter hearts and stronger nerves. They retreated, and reported; to the neighbors the strange and wonderful sounds which had greeted their ears.

Mr. Pepples laughed at the alarm of the boys, but was still on the lookout for strange sights. On last Saturday his curiosity was somewhat relieved by seeing a monster bird, something like the condor of Sinbad the Sailor, alight on his barn. It gave a few of the screams which had so disturbed the boys, and Mr. P. was satisfied he had found the ghost. He took down his rifle, and without precaution to put in a silver bullet, drew a bead, on the bird, and it fell. On approaching it he found that only one wing had been broken, which he amputated. Now comes the secret of the chains. One foot had hanging to it a steel trap weighing about four pounds, which had been evidently set for varmint. It had been there for some time, as the flesh had rotted off, the trap only hanging by a leader. On measurement, the bird proved to be seven feet from tip to tip. It was of a black color, and both similar and dissimilar in many respects to an eagle. Its feet, and the feathers of its legs, which hung about six inches in length, were those of an eagle, but the jet black color indicated another species. At last accounts it was doing well, and eating raw flesh with a voracious appetite. [6]

The community of Rabbit Hash, Kentucky, came into the news when a large bird seemingly tried to make hash of a puppy there in 1977. About 6:00 p.m. on May 16, two adult beagles and two pups were playing in the yard of Mr. and Mrs. Greg Schmidt in rural Boone County near Rabbit Hash. One of the pups, a ten-week old female weighing 5 pounds (2.3 kilograms), was picked up by a bird and carried 600 yards (549 meters) and then dropped into a pond. A neighborhood boy called it a "very big, big bird." The creature was grayish-black and had a long neck and beak. The puppy was stitched up by a veterinarian in Walton and taken home to recuperate. [7]

Before departing Kentucky, we must note that Michael Paul Henson, in a contribution to *Fate* in August 1984, related two items not recorded elsewhere. In 1950 in Lee County, he wrote, two hunters fired upon a bird with 20-foot (6-meter) wings. Further, a cliff in Johnson County was the site of a large and recently used nest found in 1970. Bird feathers 18 inches (45 centimeters) in length were also found there. [8]

Though not as large as other birds considered here, notice should be given to an enigmatic bird of prey that turned up in Ohio in 1972. Its wingspan was 5 feet (1.7 meters). Reportedly, it was identified by people at Ohio State University as an immature white-backed vulture (*Pseudogyps*) native to Africa. The bird had been shot in one wing when it was found at West Rushville, east of Lancaster. No one volunteered any explanation for this bird's appearance. [9] Incidents such as this frustrate efforts to sort out with confidence the reported appearances of unusual animals.

Both old and modern reports of huge birds exist for West Virginia as well. We are indebted to researcher Gary Mangiacopra and to Canadian researcher Mr. X (AKA Scott Poster) for being the first to find and to circulate, respectively, the location of a news report from 1895. [10] It appeared in the St. Louis (Missouri) *Globe-Democrat* on February 24. A news dispatch from Addison (now called Webster Springs) in West Virginia told of the following:

A MODERN ROC

West Virginia Mountaineers Terrorized by a
Gigantic Bird
A Ten-Year-Old Child Carried Off by the
Feathered Monster — A Hunter's Terrible
Battle —What a Deputy Sheriff Saw —
The Bird's Home

Special Correspondence of the Globe-Democrat.
ADDISON, WEBSTER COUNTY, W.VA.,
February 14.—Not since the treacherous Gauley
River rose suddenly in the night and swept scores
of the mountaineers living along its banks to
death in its icy waters, has Webster County been
so excited as it is at present. From away down on
Cherry River to the remotest settlements on Sugar
Run, in the upper part of the county, the
mountaineers are talking of the gigantic bird
which has been terrorizing this section for the
past week or ten days.

About two weeks ago a child of Dan
Junkins, who lives over on Bergoo, some fifteen
miles from this place, suddenly disappeared in a
manner which for a time puzzled the oldest
hunters and woodsmen of the county. It is now
regarded as an absolute certainty that the child, a
little girl of 10 years, fell a prey to the winged

monstrosity which for want of a better name, the mountaineers call an eagle.

Little Landy was sent by her mother one Friday afternoon to the cabin of Joe Warnick, a mile and a half south of that of Junkins, to ask after Mrs. Warnick, who had been sick. The girl started soon after noon for the Warnick cabin, but never reached there, and vanished as completely as if she had been spirited away by supernatural power. As Landy did not return by 4 or 5 o'clock, Mrs. Junkins grew uneasy, and sent her husband to look for her. He thought, perhaps, she had remained with the Warnicks, and went straight to the cabin. There he learned that the child had not been there. By that time it had become dark, and, assisted by the Warnicks, Junkins started to hunt his daughter. Nothing could be seen of her, and the whole party returned to the Junkins cabin. As there were several inches of snow on the ground, the tracks of Landy could be plainly followed. They were followed to a point within half a mile of the Warnick cabin, where they suddenly disappeared, and could not be seen any further. The point where they stopped was in a cleared field, where buckwheat had been grown last season. The child must evidently have been frightened at something for the tracks left the path, and where they stopped were some 15 to 20 feet away from it. There were a number of her tracks together, as if she had turned around and around, while trying to avoid something. Beyond this point the footprints disappeared. The search was continued far into the night, and the surrounding forest was scoured as far as possible, as it was thought the child must have wandered from the path. The searchers were compelled to return to the almost distracted mother with the news that the missing child had not been found.

The next day the search was continued by a number of others, who had heard the story, and come to volunteer their services. Search as closely as they could, beyond the footprints in the snow at the point near the path, they could not be followed further. How the child could have vanished and left no farther trace puzzled every one. If she had been seized by a wild animal, its tracks would surely have been left in the snow, but there was nothing of the kind. There was no explanation to be offered, and the mystery of the disappearance was not revealed until several days later.

A STRANGE BATTLE

Peter Swadley, a noted bear hunter of Webster, is now in the village being treated for the wounds he received from the huge bird over on Laurel Creek day before yesterday. He is still in a precarious condition from the encounter. Swadley was brought to Addison by Abe Kitsmiller on the afternoon of the day it happened. Swadley was hunting bear over on Piney Ridge, and had his dog Gunner with him. The two were tracking a bear, whose haunts Swadley had known for some days, through the laurel on the mountain side, when he came into a little clearing, and suddenly without other warning other than a scream louder than that of a panther, which Swadley thought at first had jumped on him, the immense feathered creature swooped down with the evident intention of bearing him off. The bird dug its talons in his back, tearing his coat into shreds, and for some minutes there was a fierce fight in the snow. Swadley lost his rifle, and did not get a chance to use his hunting knife. Though he is a large, powerfully built man, he had no chance with his bare hands, and his wounds show what a fight for life it must have been. One of the worst wounds the hunter received was over the left eye, where the scalp was torn away for at least three inches, making a terrible wound. Swadley still managed to retain his footing in the snow, though nearly unconscious, and strove to ward off the blows of the eagle's talons, which nearly tore him to pieces. Swadley's dog Gunner was probably the only thing that saved him from being killed. The dog was off from its master when the bird attacked him, but when Swadley shouted it returned and made for the eagle. The latter turned from the man to the dog, and Swadley says with one stroke of its powerful claws ripped open its stomach and flew away with the poor creature whining in its talons.

Almost blinded by the blood which flowed from the wound over his eye, the hunter contrived to find his way down the mountain side to the cabin of Abe Kitsmiller, on Little Laurel Creek, a mile or more from the place of conflict. He stumbled into the cabin nearly dead from the loss of blood. Kitsmiller was at home, and after he had bound up Swadley's wounds as well as he could, he put him on a horse and brought him to Addison. Owing to the fact that the bird came on him so suddenly, and nearly blinded him at the outset by the blow on the head, Swadley is not able to give much of a description of it. Its strength, however, he declares, was prodigious, and twice he was lifted off his feet by its onslaughts. Its body, he says, is as large as that of a man. "Ef it was to come as ter how I should have ter pick atwixt a painter and the varmint, in fair hand-to-hand fight, I should take the painter every time," he said telling of the affair.

A DEPUTY SHERIFF'S EXPERIENCE

Rube Nihiser, one of the County Deputy Sheriffs, who lives over on Spruce Creek, near the foot of Owl Head Mountain, and his son Hanse had a strange experience with the eagle last Thursday. Rube and his son started out in the morning on a deer hunt. As a light snow had fallen the night before it was a splendid time to track the game. They had not been out but two or three hours when they ran across the trails of a doe and fawn, and followed them around the base of the mountain, across on Piney Ridge, and down it to the laurel beds on a little branch of Sugar Run. The two hunters expected to find the deer in the beds, as they had evidently been out feeding the night before, and had gone, they thought, into the beds to rest for the day. Contrary to expectations, the tracks led through the laurel, where they were followed with difficulty into a forest of hemlocks. From the fact that the hemlock branches were so thick, and the day was so dark, it was hard to make out the trail. Nihiser knew the place well, as it was a favorite "crossing" for the deer, along

which they were accustomed to go to another laurel bed some distance away.

The two men had nearly got out of the
forest and reached a clearing which had been
made by fire burning the trees for several acres,
when they heard a terrible commotion ahead.
There were ear-splitting screams. They hurried to
the edge of the cleared spot, and 200 yards away
saw the doe and fawn with a tremendous bird of
some kind circling above them, and pouncing
down, first on one and then on the other. The bird
was of immense size, and was emitting the
screams which were heard. The doe was vainly
trying to protect the fawn. Nihiser and his son
were so astounded at the sight that they simply
stood and watched. The fawn was bleating
fearfully, and the doe was trying to ward off the
terrible attacks from the eagle. The latter would
circle up, they said, in the air 50 or 60 feet, and
then swoop down on the deer. As the two men
looked the bird suddenly wheeled down, and,
fastening its talons in the fawn's body, flapped its
wings and sailed away, apparently with ease,
over the tops of the dead trees. Nihiser put up his
rifle, and fired a departing shot without effect.
They watched the bird, which flopped its wings
until it had risen some distance up in the air, and
sailed off toward the inaccessible fastnesses of
Snaggle Tooth Knob.

The doe stood as if dazed when the men
approached, and did not attempt to move away.
It was found that the eyes had been scratched out
by the eagle's claws, and it was so badly wounded that it could hardly stand. Nihiser cut its

throat with his hunting knife, and it hide was found to be almost torn to ribbons.

Nihiser and his son say that the bird which they saw was of immense size, and that its spread of wings must have been fully 15 or 18 feet. Its body, they say, was as large as that of a man, and its cries were loud and shrill in the extreme. The feathers were of a dark brown color, with white on the wings, and light underneath. Its eyes were tremendous, larger than those of the largest-sized owl, and they shone with terrible brilliancy, plainly discernible from where they stood and watched.

HOW A SHEEP WAS STOLEN

The presence of the eagle in the county can account for in some way the inexplicable disappearance a few days ago of a sheep belonging to Hanse Hardrick from his little clearing over on Rattlesnake Run, about eleven miles north of Addison. Hardrick has a few sheep which he manages to keep through the winter. As the snow is so deep and the cold so intense this winter in Webster the sheep are kept in a bark-covered shed a few rods from the cabin. The shed is closed on all sides, and the only entrance is through a door, fronting the cabin. One morning recently Hardrick and his wife locked up the cabin and came to Addison, returning in the evening. Hardrick went to feed the sheep, when he found one of them missing. The others seemed to be frightened badly, and were huddled together in the corner of the shed. Wood was scattered all over the place, and there was a hole in the roof as if somebody had broken through. Clinging to the edges of the opening were bits of wool, which showed plainly that the sheep had been taken out that way. What puzzled Hardrick more than anything else was the fact that there were no tracks whatever anywhere about the shed, which the snow would plainly have revealed had the agency that took the sheep been, as he thought, a human one. Though not more superstitious than the rest of the mountaineers. Hardrick made up his mind that his place had been visited in his absence by a "harnt" of more than ordinary animosity.

He repaired the hole in the roof, and to prevent the return of the spirit, as is the custom of the West Virginia mountaineer, made small crosses of hemlock boughs, placed them in the shed, and nailed one over the cabin door. From what he had heard since of the eagle, he is convinced that it swooped down on the shed during his absence, tore a hole in the roof and carried away the missing sheep.

The eagle has been seen several times at a distance, by mountaineers living in the Snaggle Tooth Knob locality, and its den is evidently in the ice-bound cliffs and crags of that formidable mountain. Eph Cogar, a tenant of the Panther Cove District, which is only a few miles from the top of Snaggle Tooth Knob, for some weeks has told of a bird of gigantic proportions which he has frequently seen circling across the valley where he lives. As Eph is addicted to telling what are known in Webster as "moonshine" stories, and is also addicted to a free use of pine-top whiskey, his stories have never been credited. He avers, though, that what he has seen, "was the onerest thing in the shape of a flyin' critter I ever heerd uv befo'."

THUNDERBIRDS

A SECOND VISIT

"Pap" Tammen, one of the oldest mountaineers in Webster, says that he remembers many years ago, when the county was invaded by two just such birds as the one which is now in Webster, and that they had their den on Snaggle Tooth Knob just as this one has. He says that the creatures committed all kinds of depredations on the live stock of the people in the county, and that they remained in the haunts until the winter was over, when they disappeared and were never heard of again. This bird may be one of those which visited Webster then and has returned to its former haunts. Such a powerful creature would likely live many years. Why it has made both visits to Webster in the winter season is a mystery, as is everything else concerned about this modern counterpart of the traditional roc.

Things have come to such a pass that the Websterites are at a loss what to do. Mindful of the fate which befell the little Junkins girl, children are kept closely in the cabins, and the men who find it necessary to go about where there are no protecting trees keep a watchful eye upward, much in the same manner as do chickens watching for a henhawk.

Realistic in the extreme, the mountaineers have made no misnomer in their name of "Snaggle Tooth Knob." The peak, or rather the face, resembles almost exactly the crooked front tooth of a human being, one cliff overlapping another. The Knob even in summer is unapproachable, as in order to reach its summit it is necessary to scale a mass of perpendicular rocks. At this time of the year, when the cliffs are covered with sheets of ice, and the crevices, wide enough for a man to slip through, are hidden by thin coverings of snow, the undertaking would be rendered tenfold more dangerous.

Through the long, dark nights and the cheerless winter days there is a mother's heart in the Junkins' cabin heavy and aching with a terrible loss. Since the discovery was made that her little girl was most likely taken by the eagle, and carried to its bleak eyrie on the summit of one of the most elevated spots in Webster, Mrs. Junkins has scarcely eaten or slept. She speaks but little, and for the most part sits in the chimney corner staring into the fire with a vacant expression, and looking blankly at any one speaking to her. Occasionally she rises and walks hurriedly to the front window, where, its summit capped with snow, or enveloped in a hood of cloud, frown grimly down the barren crags of Snaggle Tooth Knob. What sensations she has at such times can best be realized by a mother who could imagine herself in her place.

From this story we can extract this summary of events:
• On February 1: Landy Junkins, a 10-year-old girl, disappeared.
• Prior to February 7: sheep were disturbed; a hole was torn in the roof of their shed.
• On February 7: Near Owl Head Mountain, a deputy sheriff, Rube Nihiser, and his son saw a giant eagle carry off a fawn.
• On February 12: A bear hunter, Peter Swadley, was attacked by a bird and badly clawed. His dog was carried off. The bird involved was 15 to 18 feet (4.6 to 5.5 meters) across the wings, and its body was as large as a man.

Giant birds have been heard of again in West Virginia. In

August 1978, Wyoming County residents reportedly saw a "large, unusual bird." Edward Cook described the bird he saw three days running as "a silver-blue color." He told Steve Williams of the Charleston *Daily Mail* that its wingspan was enormous. [11]

West Virginia is the location of encounters with giant owls, which turned up earlier in the folklore of the Midwestern Ozarks (in chapter 5). West Virginia doesn't have owl-related folklore, but some reports are best explained by the presence of Bighoot, a truly gigantic owl still known only to the chance observers of this creature of the night. (This topic is taken up at length in chapter 15.)

In Maryland in the 1930s, stories of a flying predator were circulated. The response at the time among journalists seems to have been to suspect each other of having invented the thing. According to a recent collector of folklore, Alyce T. Weinburg, the creature "once carried a full grown man to its lair in the mountains." It had also frightened the children of the black inhabitants in Middletown Valley. [12]

The Maryland bird was called the "snallygaster," but this name tells us little. Reminiscent of the "gyascutus" in the Ozarks, this word has had a long and checkered history, in this case both in politics and in the folklore of animals.

Near Great Notch Reservoir in New Jersey, an enormous white bird was seen on January 1, 1976, by Dr. Berthold Eric Schwartz, according to fortean researcher Jerome Clark. [13]

In New York State, the *Essex County Republican* for Thursday September 27, 1894, included the following text on a bird's visit to the area of Elizabethtown and Pleasant Valley:

> It was on Wednesday afternoon of last week that resident of this village, Joseph Denton and several companions were hunting squirrels on the bank of the Bouquet River just beyond the base ball field. Suddenly, as if by magic, a huge monster in "feather form" appeared over the river and only a few rods distant, from Joseph

and his companions. Joseph was the first to sight the wonderful creature, and gave his companions immediate knowledge of what he had discovered, saying "Get your guns ready, the Devil is coming."

The "bird" for such it was according to Joseph's account was big as a cow and had lungs like barn doors. It evidently was startled at the sight of man as it started to hurry but couldn't. It was so big, Joseph says the bird made as much noise going through the air as a train of cars would coming up Western Station and that its wings when spread reached from shore to shore of the beautiful Bouquet River.

When someone suggested to Joseph Denton that the bird might have been a crane, the *Republican* reported his sarcastic response that "a crane would be a mere chickadee beside that bird." The item concluded with familiar and sobering sentiments: "The strange bird and its still stronger performances were witnessed by Joseph on Wednesday and Thursday of last week. On both of these days he saw the bird only a few rods distant from him, had a loaded gun in his hand but didn't care to shoot for fear that the bird might resent the petty attack of a frail man like himself enough to swoop down, fasten on to him and carry him away to unknown parts and there to pick his bones." [14]

Modern New York has seen reports like the one made by a pilot in May of 1961. A wire service report described the experience of an anonymous private pilot who observed a bird over the Hudson River Valley, a story cited by Jack Pearl.

In 1973, Judith Diliberto had the lucky experience to sight one of the birds in northern New York in Franklin County. This happened on a farm near Chateaugay. She was walking her dog on a spring morning when she spied a bird standing in a pond. The blue-gray bird showed a wingspan of 25-30 feet (7.6-9.2 meters) when it took off. It flew north toward Canada. Here, in her own words, is how the sighting went:

> My little German Shepherd puppy had had an unfortunate encounter with a porcupine the day before so when she woke me at 5:30 to go outside I thought I had better go with her. As we walked down the dirt road from our house we walked past a pond that is quite full in the springtime. We both stopped in our tracks because we saw an immense blue-gray (battleship gray) birds standing in the pond. I would say the wingspan was 25-30 feet [7.6-9.2 meters] when it later took off. I immediately assumed with some excitement that I was seeing some endangered species that was probably living in some Canadian game preserve. I remember looking down at its legs when it flew off to see if it had an identifying bracelet of the sort that ornithologists use to mark bird. I didn't see anything. After a few moments of looking at each other, the birds unfurled its immense wings very leisurely and took off very leisurely. I watched until it was out of sight flying north toward Canada. It flew low and I was struck by the leisurely manner in which it flapped its wings. I wasn't frightened at the time but perhaps I should have been. [15]

The following year, in September, western Quebec was the scene of sightings; they took place at the village of Louvicourt near Val-D'or in the Abitibi region of Quebec. In a period of three days in 1974, from September 14 to 16, a large bird was repeatedly seen by Daniel Caron, his sister Suzette, and Remi Bessette. Daniel Caron first came upon the bird when it was drinking at a waterhole of stagnant water. Later it was seen flying over off with a dead beaver. The whitish-gray bird was 4 feet (1.2-meters) tall. The wingspread was so great the observers didn't want to go on record with the size. [16]

In New England, the birds were noticed in the 17th century by an Englishman, John Josselyn (fl.1638-1675). He recorded this description for them:

> The Pilhannaw or Mechquant much like the
> description of the Indian Ruck, a monstrous great
> Bird, a kind of Hawk, some say an Eagle, four
> times as big as a Goshawk, white Mail'd, having
> two or three purple Feathers in her head as long
> as Geeses Feathers they make Pens of, the Quills
> of these Feathers are purple, as big as Swans
> Quills and transparent; her Head is as big as a
> Childs of a year old, a very Princely Bird; when
> she soars abroad, all sorts of feathered creatures
> hide themselves, yet she never preys upon them,
> but upon Fawns and Jaccals. She ayries in the
> Woods upon the high hills of Ossapy, and is very
> rarely or seldome seen. [17]

The "high hills of Ossapy" would be the Ossipee Mountains located in east-central New Hampshire.

While the eastern part of the U.S. and Canada has been the location of much Thunderbird activity, Pennsylvania has contributed the most to the record of Thunderbirds in the East. We will next take up those accounts.

CHAPTER 9

Pennsylvania Thunderbirds

IN THE 19TH CENTURY, THE FAMOUS PAINTER JOHN James Audubon traveled by coach from Philadelphia to Mauch Chunk (now the town of Jim Thorpe), 25 miles (40 kilometers) north of Allentown. He continued on by cart beyond Mauch Chunk to observe wildlife in a land known as the Great Pine Swamp of Pennsylvania or as the Great Pine Forest. [1] The former name is of special interest because patches of swamp were to be found all across northern Pennsylvania in the forest-covered mountains. I have wondered if the swamp's presence and survival have contributed to the survival of Thunderbirds in this region. Since the Thunderbirds have been talked about for over a century in this area, the swampy places might be prime hunting ground for them. Also in this region, some enormous wingspans have been reported, beyond the 20 to 30 feet (6 to 9 meters) reported elsewhere.

For two centuries the forests of northern Pennsylvania have been known collectively as the Black Forest. In the 1920s, naturalist John W. Harshberger described the Black Forest as "3000 square miles [7770 sq. km.] of coniferous (hemlock) and hardwood forest covering a hilly country." The great forest was spread over the counties of Cameron, Clinton, Elk, Lycoming, McKean, Potter, Tioga, and Warren. [2] After 200 years of lumbering and burning off cover for agriculture, the region is now covered by regrowth and small areas of original forest. Modern maps of Pennsylvania show two large areas of formally designated forests there. The Allegheny National Forest covers parts of Warren, McKean, Forest, and Elk counties. To the south of it some virgin forest can be visited in Cook Forest State Park on the Clarion River. [3] To the east of the National Park, a collection of state forests sprawls across Cameron, Clinton, Potter, Tioga, and adjoining counties. From the heart of this second area have come most of the detailed modern accounts of Thunderbirds.

There could well be a bias toward this part of the state due to the presence of four men who have helped to build the Thunderbird record in the 20th century.

We find the best record of Thunderbirds in Pennsylvania thanks to the work of Robert Lyman Sr. Stretching from the Delaware River to the shore of Lake Erie, Pennsylvania seems to offer up an endless supply of history, folklore, and genuine wonders. Lyman made the effort to chronicle much of this material as a local historian living in Coudersport in Potter County. Potter, Cameron, and Clinton counties occupy the crumpled and forested landscape of the Allegheny Plateau in the north-central part of the state. Cameron County has remained 95 percent forested into modern times.

Lyman was the author of four books. He described the Thunderbirds in *Amazing Indeed: Strange Events in the Black Forest, Volume 2*, published in 1973. [4]

This writer was fortunate to have spent a day with Robert Lyman in the spring of 1973. We talked of the Thunderbirds, about the deer that were a nuisance in his garden, and of the other wildlife in the Pennsylvania woods that he knew so well from his years working in the forest products industries. He took me to see the famous Coudersport Ice Mine, and we talked about local history, so much of which has been preserved in his four books. [5] He pointed out that Coudersport had once been a daily stopping place for busloads of people traveling across the country, as in an era of simple roads and inexpensive bus travel, the most direct route from Chicago to New York City had been through Coudersport. Airplane travel and Interstate Route 80 many miles to the south had changed all that.

He told me about his own sighting of a Thunderbird some 30 years earlier. The bird was observed on and then over a road north of Coudersport. By measuring the road he knew its wingspread was at least 20 feet (6 meters). The creature flew off through—not over—the dense woods. This recalls the amazing ability demonstrated by some animals, such as moose with a large rack of antlers, to move with ease through dense vegetation.

Lyman's efforts revealed that the earliest surviving knowledge of Thunderbirds in the Black Forest paralleled the experience of Gladwell Richardson ("Maurice Kildare") in Oklahoma. Richardson first heard of his bird when sick in bed and tended by an elderly relative. In 1910, Calvin Carpenter was sick in bed and heard pioneer stories from Mrs. Elvira Ellis Coats, including stories about the Thunderbirds that were known to the Indians of Pennsylvania. The Indians didn't bother the birds. Later, other early settlers told Carpenter of seeing them.

Lyman was able to put together accounts that started in the 1890s and ran up to 1971. Birds had been seen in various circumstances, such as picking up a fawn, plucking an animal from in front of a car, and flying over many Black Forest locations.

The birds have been reported since then. One of the best modern accounts of a Thunderbird in the Black Forest was an observation made by Joseph and Wanda Kaye in March 1973. They once mentioned a bird frightening people in a car. What the bird is probably doing is using the draft of air from the moving vehicle for assistance in getting airborne. As already described, the birds have been reported to struggle when getting off the ground. Here is how Wanda Kaye described their experience in a letter to me:

> We saw a large object ahead of us on the right
> berm of the road. At first—as we drove toward
> it—we couldn't identify it but both my husband
> and I saw it. Then it started toward us and we
> realized it was a huge bird. Its wings were so big
> it had trouble getting off the ground. The wings
> flapped slowly and heavily as it drew abreast of
> our car. The one wing swept our windshield as it
> rose very slowly. I could see white feathers on the

head and on the feet—body appeared to be black—rather like a bald eagle—as it came even with my side car window. It seemed too heavy to get off the ground. Then we were past it and it disappeared over the trees. We were so awe-struck at the whole thing that we could hardly speak. [6]

The possible relationship of Thunderbirds to disappearances of people in the Black Forest was not a point made by Lyman in reporting on the birds. But his research on the Black Forest included 11 cases of total disappearances that have occurred there over a period of 100 years. Other tragic mishaps might have been responsible, but the cold statistics drawn from his research show that eight children and three adults disappeared without a trace of remains.

One of the earliest of Lyman's accounts might have aroused scientific interest. Fred Murray had recalled to Lyman that birds seen in 1892 got into the news. As a result, wrote Lyman, "an ornithologist from Pittsburgh came to Murray's lumber camp to observe them. He said similar birds had been seen in remote parts of West Virginia and Kentucky." While the record as we know it today is spotty, it does support this statement. However, if this ornithologist did exist, no name has survived to identify him.

Gerald Musinsky has suggested that this might have been Walter Edmond Clyde Todd (1874–1967), author of *Birds of Western Pennsylvania* (1940) and *Birds of the Labrador Peninsula and Adjacent Areas* (1980). As a young man in 1892, Todd already had a professional position in ornithology with the U.S. Department of Agriculture. He went on to a distinguished career in the field as a curator of ornithology with the Carnegie Museum in Pittsburgh. If he took an interest in Thunderbirds, nothing else has yet been found to make the connection.

Other people who contributed to the history of Keystone birds were journalist John D. Rasmussen, Clyde Mincer, and Hiram Cranmer.

In 1977, I visited Jersey Shore, Pennsylvania, and talked with John D. Rasmussen, a regional editor for the Lock Haven (Penna) *Express*. His column, "This'N'That," had carried many Thunderbird reports. He told me the birds had not made any news for two years, and he thought people had convinced themselves that they might be wrong about what they were seeing. He cited the difficulties of human observations, such as gauging distance and scale and the tricks of poor and odd lighting. He said he had a problem deciding what to print as fact. As an example, he mentioned a local citizen who had run for political office. This person had told Rasmussen that while driving to a community north of Jersey Shore, he'd seen a large bird, with an estimated wingspan of 11 or 12 feet (3.4 or 3.6 meters).

Clyde W. Mincer and his wife, Anna, also resided in Jersey Shore, on the banks of the West Branch of the Susquehanna River. They had seen the birds and Mr. Mincer passed along everything he read about the birds in the *Express* to Robert Lyman. In 1977, Mincer told me in a letter: "My wife and I have sighted twenty-five to thirty of these birds between November 1970 and December 13, 1973. None since. Three times we saw two in the air at the same time. We are on the West Branch of the Susquehanna River and see lots of big birds but no more in the twenty-foot [6-meter] range." [7]

A fourth person who had a lot to say about Thunderbirds in Pennsylvania was Hiram Cranmer, seemingly a lifelong resident of the Kettle Creek area. He had seen the birds for himself and he knew others who had. Like other people with stories to tell, he wrote to *Fate* magazine several times in the 1950s and 1960s. He wasn't a frequent observer of the birds, but his unforgettable sightings were told in the pages of *Fate* and reached more people that way than any other reports had.

Cranmer was also the source of some extravagant tales regarding local history in the Black Forest. Robert Lyman found he had a tendency to take a subject with some basis in fact and embellish it, but Cranmer's recollections and claimed sightings are only a small part of the Pennsylvania Thunderbird record.

It's easy to dismiss Cranmer's assertion that Thunderbirds are "supposed to carry off and eat 50 or more people in the United States yearly." No one is or has been in possession of enough knowledge of the birds to support such a statement. However, because of the record presented in chapter 4, I am less inclined to deny the possibility of truth in his subsequent statements. As he wrote to *Fate*, "I personally have known seven people the thunderbird has carried off. Its victims range in age from 75-year-old Barney Pluff who was devoured in 1941 to a four-year-old girl in McKean County, Pa., who was snatched in 1937 while her family was picking berries." [8]

The fear of Thunderbirds figured in a recollection of his from Hammersly Fork, a community on Kettle Creek. When Cranmer was a schoolboy, 19-year-old Thomas Eggleton disappeared. One evening in August 1897, the young man walked to the store in Hammersly Fork to mail a letter and wasn't seen again. His tracks led to a bridge over Kettle Creek and ended there. A search involving many capable trackers couldn't find him.

The people around Hammersly Fork had heard of the Indian legends of the Thunderbirds, giant birds that were a menace to large animals and human beings alike. Cranmer recalled that, after Eggleton's disappearance, the fear of them caused schools to close for two weeks. Children were afraid of walking to school. Cranmer put it this way: "I was one of them and many times I ran headlong into the house when I saw a large bird in the sky."

But Thomas Eggleton wasn't dead. Four years later, a letter arrived from South Africa, where Eggleton had been living all that time. He had suffered amnesia until a head injury in the Boer War brought back his memory of having lived in Pennsylvania; even he did not know how he came to suffer amnesia and to live in South Africa. [9]

A characteristic of genuine wonders is that they keep coming back even though some people want to dismiss them as nonexistent. In Pennsylvania today, giant-bird reports continue. Since

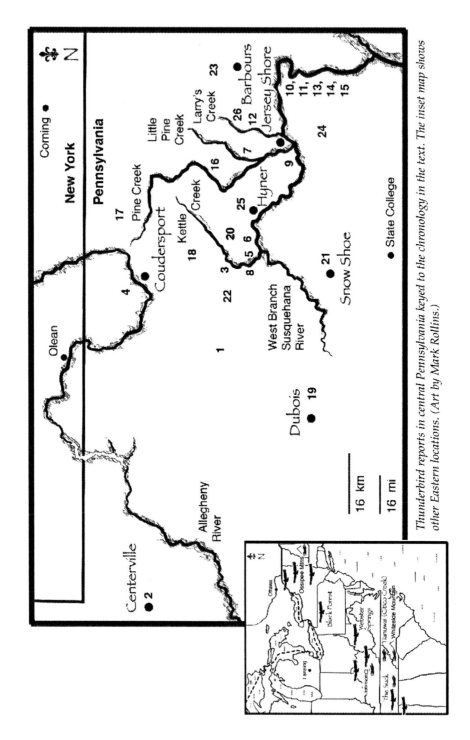

Thunderbird reports in central Pennsylvania keyed to the chronology in the text. The inset map shows other Eastern locations. (Art by Mark Rollins.)

Lyman's day, they've been collected by such people as Paul G. Johnson, Joan Jeffers, and Gerald Musinsky. [10]

Robert Lyman Sr. died in April 1974, leaving behind in his Black Forest books a delightful legacy of local knowledge about his native state. From his work and by the efforts of those who've followed, we know that Thunderbird reports originate most reliably in the present day in an area between Coudersport and Jersey Shore in Pennsylvania. In chronicling the Black Forest knowledge of Thunderbird reports, Robert Lyman opened the modern era of serious Thunderbird research.

What follows is a chronology of more than 100 years of bird reports where dates are known. The location and identified observers are listed first. Except where noted, these events have been drawn from the collection made by Robert Lyman, the columns of John Rasmussen, and the collections published by Gerald Musinsky.

No. 1. 1892
Near a lumber camp in Dent's Run, Cameron County
Lumbermen including Fred Murray of Westfield
A "flock" of birds was seen. Murray thought they looked like buzzards, only larger, with wingspans of 16 feet (4.9 meters) or greater.

No. 2. ca. 1898
Centerville, Crawford County
Arch P. Akeley
A large and extraordinary bird was trapped by a farmer. It was seen by Akeley, who described it to Robert Lyman as gray and over four feet tall.

No. 3. April 1922
Hammersley Fork on Kettle Creek
Hiram M. Cranmer
Cranmer first saw a bird he identified as a Thunderbird in 1922

but told no one for 35 years. He watched it fly past his home at dusk. From the dimensions of a tree it passed, he estimated its wingspan as 35 feet (10.6 meters).

No. 4. ca. 1940
Two miles north of Coudersport, Potter County
Robert R. Lyman Sr.
First observed in the middle of Sheldon Road, the bird flew into the trees beside the road. The wingspread was at least 20 feet (6 meters). The wings were no more than 1 foot (30 centimeters) wide.

No. 5. March 27 or 28, 1957
Hammersley Fork on Kettle Creek
Hiram M. Cranmer and others
A bird was seen repeatedly along Kettle Creek and around Renovo over a period of three weeks, beginning in late March. The wingspan estimate was 25 to 30 feet (7.6 meters to 9 meters). [11]

No. 6. July 4, 1962
Renovo, Clinton County
Hiram M. Cranmer and others
A bird was observed flying up and down area creeks (Hevner Run, Shintown Run, and Halls Run). [12]

No. 7. 1968 and 1969
Little Pine Creek
Mr. and Mrs. John Boyle
In each of these years a bird was seen. The second time it was observed, it landed in the creek. Its wings across the creek appeared to extend for 75 feet (22.6 meters).

No. 8. Summer 1969

Alvin R. Bush Lake on Kettle Creek

Albert Schoonover and two roadworkers

They watched a bird fly over the lake and then carry off a fawn.

No. 9. October 28, 1970

West of Jersey Shore

Mrs. Judith Dingler

While driving on Route 220, she observed a dark soaring bird that reminded her of an airplane.

No. 10. November 9 and 10, 1970

Jersey Shore

Clyde and Anna Mincer

Clyde Mincer described his experience in a letter to me this way: "If I recall correctly, it was the 9th and 10th of November 1970 when my wife and I saw the first huge bird which I said had a 22-foot [6.6-meter] wingspread, and I have not changed my mind since. My wife called to me as I was painting spouting and said to me, "Look at the funny airplane." It was riding a jet stream. While I watched it got off the stream, flopped its wings a few times very slow, and was back on the jet stream again. This bird was right over my house." [13]

No. 11. June 8, 1971

East of Jersey Shore

Linda L. Edwards and Debbie Kraft

The bird was seen beside Cement Hollow Road feeding on a dead opossum. It flapped its wings twice and took off. A wingspread of 18 feet (5.5 meters) was estimated.

No. 12. August 7, 1971

Larry's Creek

Clair E. Koons and Wilson Frederick
A giant bird was seen flying over the creek.

No. 13. September 23, 1972
Jersey Shore
Mary Missimer and her son, George
They were watching a helicopter fly to the east over the town when they also spied a huge, dark bird, which they compared to a Piper Cub airplane at a high altitude. They told Clyde Mincer it appeared to them to be skillfully riding air currents.

No. 14. September 25, 1972
Jersey Shore
At 3:10 p.m., the bird in No. 13 was observed again flying to the northwest.

No. 15. September 28, 1972
Jersey Shore
Clyde Mincer and Mary Missimer
At 11:30 a.m. at the Missimer home, they observed a big bird soaring southwest of Jersey Shore.

No. 16. March 31, 1973
Oregon Hill Ski Area, Lycoming County
Mr. and Mrs. Joseph Kaye
On Route 287, a giant bird took off from the right side of the road and became airborne over their vehicle. [14]

No. 17. August 7, 1973
Sunderlinville, Potter County
Inez Bull and Lady Johann Randulf Bull
The two women were in a car when a huge eagle-like bird flew over them. Inez Bull and her mother saw the bird. Miss Bull was director of the Ole Bull Museum at Carter Camp. (Their ancestor,

Ole Bull, was a 19th century Norwegian violinist who tried to found a Scandinavian colony in Pennsylvania.) The ladies were returning home in a Volkswagen from a dinner party in Westfield in Tioga County. They had just made a turn at Sunderlinville in Potter County when this bird took off from the left side of the road. When spread, its wings reached from one side of the road to the other. John Rasmussen quoted Miss Bull as saying, "It flew against the side of the vehicle, swiped at the front end and tried to attack it." She accelerated the car, which she felt allowed them to escape. Her mother was upset, saying, "I thought it was going to eat us."

No. 18. October 14, 1973

Cross Fork Creek

Several observers as indicated below.

I will introduce this episode with a paragraph written by Robert Lyman in a letter to me in February 1974: "My son, his wife, and six others saw three Thunderbirds last fall fly over their camp on Cross Fork Creek. Bob Jr. is 52 years old. He has been going to that camp all his life and never before sighted such a bird. How can the reference books all agree there is no such bird? The ignorance of good minds in high places is truly amazing." [15]

John Rasmussen reported in his newspaper column that these sightings occurred on October 14. He took his information from a letter to the Mincers written by Robert Lyman Sr. On that date, Bob Jr. and his wife Mary Ellen observed two huge birds fly up the valley of Cross Fork Creek at about 1:00 p.m. Shortly thereafter, nine guests arrived at the camp. Two of the younger men climbed a steep and high mountain by the camp, taking a walkie-talkie with them. From the top of a cliff, they saw a big bird flying down the valley and alerted the camp with their hand radio set. Others saw this same bird fly by. Bill Good was one of the men on the cliff. Lyman wrote to the Mincers: "Bill said the bird was at about the same elevation as the point he stood on the rocky precipice, and the huge thing flew by only a few hundred feet away." Bill Good remarked upon the slow movement of the bird's wings as it flew. This bird was gray in color and had a wingspan of at least 15 feet (4.6 meters).

No. 19. Spring 1977
Nine miles south of DuBois
Debbie Wright and Sue Howell
On Route 219, these two schoolteachers saw something Sue Howell described this way: "It was big, black or very dark brown, with a huge beak."

No. 20. August 1977
Donut Hole Trail, Sproul State Forest, Clinton County
Terry McCormick
While hiking, he saw a bird the size of a Piper Cub airplane.

No. 21. May or June 1978
Near Snow Shoe, Centre County
Herb Nesman
While working on an oil derrick, Nesman observed something he took to be a small airplane. When the thing flapped its wings, he realized it was a bird with a wingspan that might have been more than 18 feet (5.5 meters). [16]

No. 22. 1989
Sinnemahoning area, Cameron County
Anonymous camper
Paul G. Johnson reported that this person observed "a huge bird with a 'funny-looking' beak sitting in a tree. It was between 4 and 5 feet [1.2 and 1.5 meters] in height and completely brown-colored." [17]

No. 23. November 1989

Barbours, Lycoming County

Shannon Breiner

On a relative's farm she saw a "large, eagle-like bird" that ran into a swamp. It was, she said, "not a frail bird."

No. 24. Late September 1992

North White Deer Ridge, southern Lycoming County

Kim Foley

Driving home in the afternoon, she saw a bird eating a deer. The bird was bigger than a Stellar's Sea Eagle. "It was huge and dark brown, almost black" with an "ugly beak," she said.

No. 25. October 1992

Near Hyner, Clinton County

Dave Sims and his two sons, Zach and Casey

Sims said that "it was a big, dark gray bird" that flew faster than he was driving.

No. 26. July 1993

Larry's Creek

Shane Fisher and his parents observed a large bird above the trees on their property. It was described as "eagle-like." Eyes were large and black. Wings were "wider than a crossbar on a telephone pole."

While this sample is small, there is a noteworthy absence of reports for the months of December, January, and February. In fact, the reports occurred from the very end of March into early November. Clyde Mincer, in a letter quoted earlier, gave a date of December 13, 1973, for his last sighting, but we have only a date without any additional information about his observation.

The absence of bird sightings for almost five months might be due to (1) less outdoor human activity in the colder months, (2) less activity by the birds in those months, or (3) the departure of the birds from the area altogether.

The wintertime appearances of giant birds historically observed in West Virginia give some support to the last possibility. What is suggested by reports for the Thunderbirds from Quebec, New York, and points southward is that the birds are engaging in a seasonal migration, southward in the winter and northward in the warm months. Pennsylvania, with its forests and swamps, appears to offer a place where the big birds will linger and might be seen by a lucky few.

CHAPTER 10

A Bird of Prey

MY OPINION IS THAT MUCH OF THE MATERIAL PRE-
sented in previous chapters can be explained by the existence of a
gigantic bird of prey now living in North America. Putting aside the
distinctive reports of "Bighoot" for the present, a description can be
drawn from the most detailed of the remaining bird encounters. A
hypothetical sketch of its habits and migration patterns can be made
from the bulk of the various sources.

A consideration of the quality of the foregoing record of legend and lore and the fate of the alleged physical evidence for the
birds will be taken up in the next chapter.

The bird is distinguished by its size and lifting capabilities
exceeding those of any known bird living today anywhere in the
world. Wingspan estimates are necessarily all guesswork. But
observers sometimes have had the benefit of a measurable object for
comparison or the benefit of time to observe a resting bird. The
results most often have provided sizes of 15 to 25 feet (4.6 to 6
meters). The bird at rest or on the ground appeared to be 4 to 8 feet
(1.2 to 2.4 meters) tall. A rare instance of dimensions for the
American Indian Thunderbird appeared in a tale collected by
George Laidlaw that was published in 1916. He wrote: "This was a
big monster eagle with wings about twenty feet [6 meters] long and
body about eight feet [2.4 meters] wide." [1]

Typically, the coloring of the birds is dark: brown, gray, or
black. The Illinois birds in 1977 had a white ring on the neck. The
head and neck are usually bare. This fact helps explain the descriptions given in 1948 and also the appearance of the bird in the Huffer
film. The head and neck are sometimes hard to see against the back-
ground of the sky, which is why the bird has sometimes appeared
to witnesses to be headless. White wing tips are sometimes men-

tioned. Robert Lyman suggested that the Pennsylvania birds changed from brown to gray as they matured. [2]

The size of its living prey makes this an unusual bird. The animals it kills for food include sheep, deer, caribou, moose, colts, dogs, whales (according to one source, the "killer" and finback whales [3]), and, by widespread accounts, human beings. One critic of Thunderbirds has complained that the birds have nothing to eat. There seems to be plenty for these birds to feast upon in the wild and in those places where domestic animals can be found. Also mentioned in the course of this book are other prey, including beaver, bison, elk, antelope, pigs, and cattle. The birds appear to be opportunists, at least in historical times, taking whatever animals come into view.

While the outward appearance of the Thunderbird is often compared with the California condor, its traits match up well with the larger species found in another order in the same family, the hawks. For example, they are hunters of live prey. One gender is larger than the other (the larger individual is the female). They possess a decurved bill and gripping feet. They breed on crags, in simple nests of sticks and leaves. They have one or two eggs in a nest. In keeping with the shared traits then, they are likely to be long-lived and slow breeding. Also, they may return to the same nests each year. [4]

Among raptors, the female is often larger than the male. This difference in size tends to ensure that the young will be fed in the nest. Also, the larger of the two adults is the one that guards the nest. Each gender can take different kinds of prey. [5] Whether Thunderbirds take different prey according to their sex is not yet clear.

Thunderbird stories of the American Indians give two as the number of young in the nest with only two exceptions. From the lore of the Micmac, Malecite, Ojibwe, Potawatomi, Menominee, Cherokee, and Blackfoot, the number is two. James Mooney related two stories from the Cherokee, the first with two young birds and the second with four young ones. [6] Also, Dorothy M. Brown related that on one summertime visit to Thunder Mountain in

Wisconsin, the Potawatomi were surprised to see "several pairs" of the young birds instead of the usual two. [7] The color of the young when mentioned is brownish red or white.

Noteworthy sounds produced by the Thunderbirds include the roar of the wings in flight and some distinctive vocalizations. In 1899, Edward Nelson took note of the "noise like thunder" that Eskimos attributed to the moving wings of the birds. [8]

A witness to a bird in Illinois in July 1977, James Majors, said the noise he heard "sounded like a jet taking off." [9] Also in Illinois that year, "Texas John" Huffer complained that the bird made an awful sound, a "kind of a clacking sound." He found its "weird cry" to be "primeval." [10]

Here we can recall the vocalization of a bird reported by Merle Rose in Amarillo, Texas, which, as it rested, made a "whoo, whoo, whoo" sound. [11]

Despite the noises produced by the Thunderbirds, the birds seem capable of quiet flight when approaching potential prey, a characteristic brought out in some accounts. For example, in Oklahoma in the 1800s, Gladwell Richardson's bird was notorious for surprising its potential victims. After the bird strikes, as reported by James Majors in Illinois, the wings produce thunder as the bird regains altitude.

According to Robert Lyman, gliding flight is common when Thunderbirds can take advantage of air currents. He quoted Clyde Mincer as observing a bird's soaring flight over Jersey Shore, Pennsylvania. [13] The birds welcome some assistance in getting in the air and appear to use the draft of moving vehicles when possible. This behavior has been reported in Eastern states from Tennessee to Pennsylvania.

Thunderbirds are frequently observed resting in trees for up to five minutes, as near Odin, Illinois, in 1977. Other instances occurred at Eastbay, California, at Winnemucca, Nevada, and at Amarillo and Montalba in Texas. This frequency suggests that for the birds, flight can be quite tiring and rest stops may be essential where gliding isn't convenient. The use of moving vehicles for assistance in getting aloft has given the birds a bad reputation. People feel as if they are being attacked when the Thunderbirds fly low over their automobiles looking for assistance in getting off the ground.

As their stamina may be questionable, so may be their individual lifting capabilities. The remarkable size of their prey is often emphasized in tales involving caribou, whales, and adult humans as their victims. But the creatures also are said to carry off beavers, colts, pigs, dogs, and even puppies. Taking into consideration all the folklore and other accounts, the birds seem to show a preference for children over adults in humans as prey. While some Thunderbirds may be capable of taking very large prey, it's likely that all the birds are not created equally in this respect. Perhaps very few are capable of heavy lifting.

Having proposed a greater threat to young people than to adults from Thunderbirds, here may be the place to address the general danger to humans from such birds.

The outdoors contains hazards. There are risks, such as getting lost and encountering a bear. But people adjust to these dangers by having knowledge and acting prudently. Some people do not adjust, of course, and they become lost and are injured by bears. But the awareness of a risk—here a slight one to humans from a rare predatory bird—should be enough of a guide for most people. In Illinois in the summer of 1977, it would have for been fair warning and a healthier situation for the population to know that a genuine risk did exist for a brief period.

Knowledge is preferable to confusion and to vulnerability due to ignorance. People do not panic when other natural forces threaten, such as storms, tornadoes, and the like. They want to be given fair warning. It could be said that one reason to tackle the mystery of giant bird reports is to help determine where and when a genuine risk exists from these birds. The risk for humans probably increases when food for the birds is scarce. The scarcity of game was a condition during the period that Blood Indians were preyed upon in Alberta in the 1800s. Marlon Lowe may have been nearly victimized because of the lack of other food for the migrating birds in the modern landscape of central Illinois.

The events in Illinois in 1977 also indicate that the birds have a mobility that permits them to range widely in North America. Their basic needs might be summarized as something to eat and a tree to rest in. Sightings of the birds require people to be awake to see them in enough light to observe their unusual appearance. With these restrictions in mind, we note that reports from Illinois have come early in the day and in the evening hours. In all likelihood, the birds migrate at night, as do many other birds.

A continent-wide familiarity with Thunderbirds is found among the American Indians and Eskimos of the past. In the Great Lakes area, the birds even nested year after year in accessible locations that were visited by the Indians. Elsewhere, in mountainous regions, the birds are reported to choose the most inaccessible sites for their nests. The birds are clearly fewer in number than they were centuries ago. As long as any number of them survive, we can expect them to continue to live by the habits they have known for thousands of years in the post-Pleistocene world.

The birds we can identify as North American Thunderbirds have appeared throughout the continent. Some have taken this to indicate that they cannot be real. However, the distribution of these birds is not unusual and the habits they exhibit are what would be expected of birds of this kind. The habits that are indicated by the known reports and the Indian lore are those of a migratory bird of prey. The birds are annually on the move in the East, in the Central states, and in the West.

The birds have appeared in the East during the warm months of the year in places from Pennsylvania to Quebec. During the winter, they aren't seen in the north, but they've been reported in West Virginia in February. Further south, the lore and nesting sites are numerous, suggesting they have always been known in the Southeastern states.

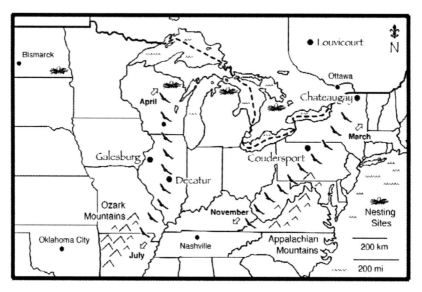

Reports indicate the birds are migrating annually from south to north and back.
(Art by Mark Rollins.)

The birds are seen in Pennsylvania from late March into early November. In the fall, they have been seen as far north as Quebec. It seems likely that in spring, when they must find their way north from the southern regions, one route takes them into Canada. This route is by way of the Hudson River Valley, then Lake Champlain, and perhaps along the Ottawa River on their way deep into Quebec. It should be kept in mind that the birds will be migrating at night so that their likely detection along such a route will be lessened.

Whether the birds still have destinations in the Northeast other than Quebec and Pennsylvania is not clear. We can only say we lack modern reports of birds that are clearly Thunderbirds. There are other winged mysteries (e.g., Bighoot) that must be allowed for when reports are vague; these vague reports exist for New England.

The north-south route of Thunderbirds that appear in the Keystone State might be hypothesized by connecting the Black Forest with the area of West Virginia where the birds were known to appear in the 1800s. Birds that rely on gliding flight are likely to

THUNDERBIRDS

follow such north-south-trending mountains as Chestnut Ridge and Laurel Hill. Also conducive to such traffic would be the fact that this area is the least populous part of the state. These birds seem to like places where people are few. Following either ridge would seem to funnel the birds into the valley of the Cheat River in West Virginia. This is perhaps the best place to look for the regular migration of the birds in the East. From there, the birds would have an easy flight to central West Virginia. They have been identified as nesting in points further south in Kentucky, North Carolina, and Tennessee.

Most of these nesting sites have been mentioned already (Citico Creek, Whiteside Mountain, Johnson County in Kentucky). Another site associated with a Thunderbird nest is The Suck, where Suck Creek meets the Tennessee River near Chattanooga. [13]

The continued appearances of the birds in the Central states such as Illinois and Missouri have caused much consternation, especially among ornithologists who cannot stomach the possibility of large birds flying over this territory. Nevertheless, the birds continue to migrate just as they certainly have for thousands of years. In the East and in the West, the birds are sheltered by mountains. In the Central states, this is not the case when the birds fly north in the spring and when they are returning southward. It's natural, then, that they would be seen more often in this area, despite their movements during nighttime migration. This could explain the bird sightings in 1948 and 1977. In the 19th century, a bird appeared in July at Mulberry Grove, Illinois, just as two birds appeared at Lawndale, Illinois, in July 1977. They were migrating south on a long-used route to Southern mountains.

What we see today of the central migration route is almost certainly but a remnant of what it once was. In the fresh post-Pleistocene environment, the birds probably over-wintered in the mountains of the southern Plains. There is a tier of mountains in Arkansas and Oklahoma; these highlands are the Wichita, Arbuckle, Ouachita, and Boston mountains. In the spring, the birds would have flown north to an area stretching from the Black Hills to the Great Lakes. This arrival in the spring accounts for the birds in this part of the continent being identified as Thunderbirds. Their reappearance coincided with the return of thunderstorms to the northland. When the wings of the birds produce such thunderous sounds, it isn't surprising that they would become closely associated with these storms.

In the north, the birds in the distant past would have found a world of vast, shallow, and dying lakes. These were remnants of the great ice cap that once rested on North America. Such glacial lakes as Agassiz and Dakota departed slowly from the middle of the continent, according to Indian traditions. Also, the Indians have said, the lakes were inhabited by large snake-like creatures. These "serpents" were known to be deadly enemies of the Thunderbirds. The American Indians called the water dwellers "Uktena" and other similar names. [14] These creatures are another animal mystery awaiting resolution and merit their own discussion elsewhere in the future. Such things have been described not so long ago; an example of which is a serpent-like monster reported in Lake Michigan in 1867. [15]

The birds have been repeatedly observed standing in shallow bodies of water, perhaps both drinking and cooling down from periods of stressful flight. This habit suggests they would have been likely to encounter the Plains serpents at such times.

The American Indians have identified across this territory particular high points of land with the birds. In the days of the thundering herds of bison and the giant serpents, the Thunderbirds used to nest nearby and take their prey as needed in the plains and the forests of the north.

The birds were known to nest on Harney Peak, the highest point in the Black Hills. [16] Devil's Nest in North Dakota was named for the birds that made it a roosting place. A region of rough terrain located in Nebraska also bears the name of Devil's Nest. Its high point is 450 feet (137 meters) above the surrounding bottom land. [17] It would be helpful to know the antiquity of the name. Did the Indians supply the label, perhaps for the same reason as the other "Nest"? Or was it simply named for its later use as an outlaw hideout?

Around Lake Superior, we find locations that might still be

visited by Thunderbirds. This region was either the destination or on the route of birds migrating through Illinois, as in the 1977 episode. On the northern shore of the lake, these special birds were known to be found by the Mississauga Indians of the past. [18] As noted earlier, Mt. McKay in Ontario was identified as a nesting place. [19]

To the south of Lake Superior, the birds are associated with certain heights of land. According to Dorothy Moulding Brown in her discussion of Wisconsin legends: "In the rugged mountains of the Penokee Iron Range near Hurley in Iron County, in the former domain of the Chippewa Indians, were the reputed nesting places of the Thunderers (wassamowin—lightning makers)." [20]

Thunder Mountain in Wisconsin's Marinette County is a story-rich prominence known to the Potawatomi and the Menominee Indians as a nesting place. The nests and eggs of the bird were seen there often. A pond on the mountain was associated with a water serpent that battled the Thunderbird. [21]

Further south in Wisconsin, we also find traces of the birds. At Fox's Bluff, on the north shore of Lake Mendota, the Winnebago said there was a roosting place of the birds. They stopped there "on their long flights from their nesting places on the high mountains on the shore of Lake Superior." [22]

The birds' movements were suggested in this bit of Menominee folklore: "I-na-maq-ki, the Big Thunder, lived at Winnebago Lake, near Fond-du-Lac. The Good Spirit made the Thunderers the laborers and to be of benefit to the whole world. When they return from the southwest in the spring they bring the rains which make the earth green and cause the plants to grow." [23]

As one who is always looking for the connections between folklore and natural phenomena, I see the possible association of Thunderbirds with the origin of "The Night Rider" known in Fond-du-Lac County. [24] This legend, as told in *Wisconsin Lore*, is long on atmospherics and short on specifics. It tells of an aerial menace that has been reported on occasion. Stories of this noisy aerial phantom may have originated with the passing of the Thunderbirds.

Even further south, in Illinois, we have the modern accounts of birds already cited to reveal to us the birds' route. From around Caledonia in the north all the way to Lake Shelbyville, the birds have been reported along the same route in different years. This is the western edge of the morainic glacial deposits left after the end of the Pleistocene. The birds are following the edge of the Marengo Ridge, the Bloomington Morainic System, and the Shelbyville Morainic System. Going north in April and south in July, the birds have probably followed this route for thousands of years.

When I was able to examine the appearances of the birds on the DeLorme *Illinois Atlas & Gazetteer* in conjunction with other maps of geographical data, it was readily apparent that most of the reports fell at the western edge of these major geological features. [25]

Repeated sightings at Galesburg might indicate another route connecting with the Mississippi River, or the birds might simply deviate temporarily in search of food. In 1977, the birds appear to have deviated briefly from this route by simply following Kickapoo Creek eastward to the area of Downs and Bloomington. Locations such as Lawndale and Waynesville are at the very edge of the moraine.

The higher and hilly moraines have been worn down over time while the territory to the west has been and remains flat. Approaching Peoria from the west on Interstate 74, a driver will notice this change in topography when nearing the Brimfield-Oak Hill turnoffs. This is a road-cut for the Interstate and the terrain becomes elevated.

Landmarks the birds and their ancestors knew, such as Winnebego Swamp, which once filled the southwestern corner of Lee County, are now gone. The swamp has been ditched and drained. But the birds are still seen, as we know, at Caledonia, Lawndale, Waynesville, Decatur, and Lake Shelbyville. From the reservoir they follow the Kaskaskia River southwestward toward the Ozarks, where they are also recorded.

If the 1977 reports are typical, the trip southward is made

in July and early August. The birds in the Midwest have a more difficult trip than in the East and West, where there are mountains and updraft to go with them. Perhaps the warmer season and prehistoric availability of prey were factors in determining the timing of migration in the central states.

The birds appear in Texas and Oklahoma in the colder months; of course, more reports would be welcome to determine the birds' habits. At this point, we can only work with what we have, bits of folklore from Missouri and Arkansas that suggest where the birds might over-winter. They are identified with Christian, Greene, and Howell (West Plains) counties in Missouri. Vance Randolph refers to giant birds and associated lore there. [26] In Texas and Shannon counties, the bird was known as the Black Eagle, an enormous bird. When sighted, it was considered to be an omen. [27] In Arkansas, giant birds were at least talked of in Carroll County. [28] The mountains of Arkansas and Oklahoma seem the most likely to harbor whatever descendants of Pleistocene giants have survived into modern times.

Movement between the eastern and central ranges of today's Thunderbirds is possible. The most likely avenues for any such traffic are the Ohio River (birds at Cairo and Rabbit Hash) and the Hatchie River in Tennessee. The latter has a broad swampy bottom and it begins in Tippah County, Mississippi, where birds were reported in the 19th century.

To the east of the Hatchie River basin there are some highlands where Eddy Reese spied a bird in 1975. This terrain merges with the southern Appalachians.

The scarcity of reports in the American West is due in large part to the absence of a modern tradition of living giant birds there. And no one has spent time following up leads as has been done in the East. The wide-open spaces, mountains, deserts, and low population density play a part as well. Thunderbirds have been reported flying up the California coast, but reports haven't become part of any published record.

When they are seen, there is no obvious place to go to report such activity, and the person making the report is put in the position of having to prove his or her claim. This is a difficult task, even if you have motion film, as "Texas John" Huffer did.

Out West, the birds are seen from California to Alaska. They are likely to adjust to the seasons as other birds do. They appear further north in summer, and their range shifts southward in winter. A bird in Alaska might winter in southern Canada, while a bird in Canada might winter in California.

The picture of the Thunderbirds that emerges from the mix of folklore, personal recollections, and news accounts is a formidable creature capable of surviving into the modern day. There are far fewer of them than there once were. Flight gives it mobility to find food and choose its living space. The lack of distinctive markings and coloration today gives it a healthy ambiguity among birds. In the West, the confusion with the California condor would have helped it survive undetected. The general difficulty in knowing the size of any bird in flight would also help obscure their presence.

The bird as reconstructed was once the master of the skies, but in the past 100 years it has successfully maintained itself in smaller areas. With a few exceptions, the Thunderbirds have remained unknown to the new Anglo-American and other settlers of its world. In its obscurity, this bird has so far escaped any organized effort to harm it or to help it.

I suspect the difficulty in estimating a bird's size in the air would be a basis upon which to throw out the largest reported wingspans in the Thunderbird record. Extremely large spans of 50 and 75 feet (15.2 and 22.8 meters) have been reported, from such widely separated points as Florida, Pennsylvania, and Alaska. It would be too easy a device to throw out such estimates as exaggeration and as errors in guesswork. Perhaps (that word again) they represent something distinctive, by subspecies or even by species. Such questions should be considered as more is learned about Thunderbirds. Typically, there is more wonder and diversity in nature than we can anticipate.

CHAPTER 11

A Fortean Problem

THUNDERBIRDS DO NOT YET HAVE A PLACE IN ornithology. But, like many strange animals people report, they will not go away. Thunderbirds have been sustained by American Indian traditions, by a historical and modern record of uncommon claims, and even by physical evidence, most of which has not been preserved for present-day examination.

Nevertheless, the "physical evidence" in the forms of captured and killed birds, remains of birds and their victims, and photographic proof (both motion film and still photography) should be given some consideration, if only to acquaint the reader with the kinds of evidence that might be found in the future in support of Thunderbirds. This kind of evidence has survived long enough in the past to support the judgments and beliefs of people that giant birds have existed. The photographic evidence will be taken up in chapter 12.

Much has been written here of the 1977 Illinois events because they demonstrate how an extraordinary creature such as a giant bird can manifest itself in the heart of a modern nation and still be overlooked. The science of ornithology responded to these events with an arrogant dismissal based upon superior and unspecified "zoological knowledge." [1] Such a subject is overlooked, and therefore neglected, when its appearance is dismissed or superficially explained away with no recognition of the consistency of detail, of the history of like events, and of the possibilities inherent in the variety that the natural world possesses.

Valuable detail is easily overlooked when a flood of interest brings in much useless data as well, as happened in Illinois. At the time, patient attention wasn't applied to events and to history. A historical memory for odd events is rarely maintained, and in Illinois in 1977 it was totally lacking.

A common but mistaken reaction was to force all things to be explained only in terms of the familiar. To take seriously the possibility of unfamiliar birds would have been to go against the long-established and self-perpetuating conclusion that nature can and must be explained by things already well known. The persistence of Thunderbird reports is an argument for a natural world that is vast and still poorly understood.

No organized effort to pursue the subject of Thunderbirds is known to have been undertaken. Likewise, no funds have ever been available to support research or fieldwork that could seek out and preserve evidence. Quite simply, the pursuit of Thunderbirds has never been anyone's job. The reader may recall that Vernon Kleen was assigned by the Illinois Department of Conservation to "solve the mystery." In Missouri in 1948, Charles Hartenstein, an assistant to the mayor of St. Louis, was assigned to trap "Big Bird." Were these men seriously given the time and resources to come up with an answer, especially if that answer was the one presented here? What more could be expected to come from such political buck-passing than a dismissal of the whole problem?

Oversized-bird reports, in common with other reports of unusual animals can be safely ignored. There is no long-term pressure to examine, categorize, or explain them in any way that is truly scientific, i.e., a thorough reliable and public examination subject to the scrutiny of other informed individuals.

The absence of organization, funds, and skilled dedication is common where questions of mysterious happenings occur. These are some of the characteristics of fortean problems, i.e., inquiries into topics popularly raised but not professionally pursued by scientists. Thunderbirds are typical of a fortean problem in appearing in a historical record that is fragmented and stretched over many years. Also, important events have taken place at locations widely separated geographically, making investigation even more difficult.

Other characteristic difficulties and their reflections here include:

• No reliable, widely shared information base. Because professional activity on the issue of Thunderbirds is lacking, the discussion of them has necessarily been in popular magazines such as *Saga, Fate,* and *True Frontier,* in popular books (by Lyman, Keel, and Coleman), and in fortean publications with small circulations.

• Increasing complexity when a body of information is assembled. Markedly different causes emerge among giant birds, as is already evident by the presence of both large owls and hawk-like predators.

• The absence of an active, widely known tradition. While the symbol of the Thunderbird could be termed "universally known," no active tradition exists, outside of Pennsylvania, of appearances of this bird. The existence of a widely known label, however incorrectly it may be applied (e.g., "Bigfoot," "the Loch Ness Monster"), allows more information to become known from current events and historical records.

Thunderbirds have a secure position in anthropological literature. Their importance could be explained away to the satisfactions of many anthropologists as cultural features telling us little about actual birds. Further consideration by these anthropologists involve only whether these stories were diffused or independently invented. A purpose of this book is to call for another interpretation to be considered—inspiration by genuine giant birds.

The remaining record from other than anthropological sources could be assailed as stemming from lies, hoaxes, and exaggerated tall tales told for entertainment, profit, or attention. This writer thinks it couldn't be criticized successfully in this way. Just as proof is sought to support an assertion in favor of the birds' reality, proof should be required for the kinds of charges listed here whenever they are made. To date, critics of Thunderbird reports have been unable to make any kind of case against their validity. They've fallen back upon their own whimsical prejudice that the reports are simply "impossible."

Some critics of the survival of giant birds will argue that places like West Virginia have been thoroughly examined for birdlife and that no giant birds have been found. But that simply assumes the conclusion within their argument. The issue here is whether or not that assumption is in error. "Where are the reports of giant birds?" they will ask. But that's what is presented here. Modern reports of giant birds continue. Why aren't there more of them? Three reasons: the birds are not numerous; the birds are secretive and utilize the cover of darkness and their natural camouflage well (especially in the case of Bighoot), and people are discouraged from making sightings known.

The experience of the Lowe family should be enough to make the case that ridicule is heaped upon people for telling their personal encounters with something rare and hard to capture. There is, however, additional testimony.

Here's what one veteran birdwatcher had to say in January 2003 about reporting unusual birds in Virginia:

> As a long-time birdwatcher, I have learned that even when it comes to little things, like, say, a blue-gray gnatcatcher spending the winter in Virginia, most bird authorities won't listen to you unless you file a detailed report, preferably with a good photo. I went on a Christmas bird count last year that yielded a black-and-white warbler and a gnatcatcher in Virginia during the month of December. The warbler was not taken seriously, even though it and another neotropical species had been found wintering in the same place the year before. God help someone who sees a boreal owl in Virginia.

In light of all this: I know folks who see rare owls, sandhill cranes, and the like in my neck of the woods, and don't report them at all for fear of being laughed at by other birders. I'd imagine anyone who saw a Bachman's warbler or ivory-billed woodpecker today would do the same. Even if the bird landed on your head, unless you had a good photo, not a soul would believe you. Even a respected expert in the field of ornithology would shudder at the idea of telling someone they saw one of these rare birds, especially if it were never seen again. Any evidence would be subject to ridicule. The bird in the photo is stuffed, the feather is from a pileated woodpecker or stuffed specimen, the call you heard was a starling or mockingbird's mimic, yada yada yada…. It's the same ridicule that keeps the thylacine in the shadows and lake monsters from being taken seriously by most scientists.

When these remarks were posted on a webpage with the author's name, he was given sufficient "unwanted attention" that his name had to be removed. Where freedom of speech is exercised, there are people only too eager to exercise their opportunity to harass other speakers for their views.

To say that it isn't logical for big birds to exist at this time is again putting the cart before the horse. My findings are that two kinds of giant birds are still around. It's logical for this to be so because they are but two of many kinds of creatures that are not catalogued but still exist. It is logical because this is the modern condition. Extraordinary but rare creatures are eluding us. We aren't making much effort to find them, either. It would be a fallacy to assert that we are. Instead, collectively we have been insulting and harassing the people who have been fortunate enough to see such things and speak up about them.

We should also be wary of attempts to apply incorrectly the principle of parsimony (Occam's Razor). These are appeals to bless "a simple solution." The simplest solution (no new birds here, only human failings) is not blessed by this principle as the correct answer. The principle calls for the solution that best takes into account all the circumstances involved. This book attempts to acquaint the reader with what those circumstances are. Those who argue against Thunderbirds and the like don't want to face and try to otherwise explain the extensive records in folklore and history.

As noted above, an objection sometimes made to a physical reality for Thunderbirds is that "the birds are well known." Birds are a subject of interest and fascination for virtually everyone in touch with nature. Many people, for both amateur and professional reasons, spend a lot of time studying birds. They go to great lengths to pursue, observe, and study particular species and to share their knowledge through organizations and journals. But none of this curiosity and energy has yet been directed at the species of birds proposed here. The people, the organizations, and the journals stick to their specific interests and pay no attention to these unusual birds.

The idea that reports of large birds are misidentifications of stray condors has been put forth as a way to explain them away. The Andean condor has even been suggested as a likely wanderer up from its South American haunts into North American airspace. If such events ever took place—condors from California and the southern hemisphere flying over the East—people in the bird-watching community would be delighted. They'd love to add a sighting of these magnificent birds to their life lists. When an unusual bird is found to have flown off its normal course to a foreign shore, the people do the flocking. Bird spotters travel to such events in large numbers for one of these sightings.

But such events for the condors simply haven't occurred. The birds can be a rare sight even in their normal habitats. They are rare birds and don't wander. The situation is akin to a military one. If a foreign jet comes into the airspace of the U.S., it would be detected and tracked during its travel. There is a reason to be concerned and a procedure in place to respond to the concern. At the same time, unidentified flying objects go unmolested because they are not understood and are not interpreted as a threat. In the same way, in the bird-watching world, Thunderbirds are not understood and are not recognized for what they are. So when giant birds appeared over Illinois in 1977, no one in Illinois tried to track them at the time. No effort was set into motion to follow their progress through the state.

This could change. If Thunderbirds were discussed in bird journals, which they are not, and if birders were informed about what a Thunderbird looks like, which at this time they are not, *then* the stage would be set for some productive observations of giant birds. When the birds were thought to be active, they could be tracked by good sighting reports. We might then learn something more about their appearance and habits. Until an informed approach is taken, the occurrences of giant birds will continue to be a spotty history of the birds being recognized only briefly and then disappearing back into the forests and mountains of North America.

The birds are sufficiently known that there exist fossil forms of birds clearly related to the proposed Thunderbirds and giant owls. (These "giant teratorns" and owls will be explored in chapters 14 and 15.) In the area of bird paleontology, professional scientists have made their only contributions to our subject. Why this is likely to remain the case will be taken up in chapter 16.

Mankind takes a largely selfish attitude toward its fellow animals. Birds are treated as food or put into service. If they constitute a major nuisance, they are destroyed. Thunderbirds, if they exist, do not serve mankind and, while not necessarily benign, are not a major nuisance.

As with other rare animals, some might propose that Thunderbirds have survived into recent times but may now be extinct. Counter considerations are that the birds could be adapting to modern conditions and that all life is tenacious.

Beyond stories and sightings, a variety of physical evidence has helped to persuade American Indians and others that giant birds exist. But these material things were not viewed as evidence to be preserved for posterity's benefit. Most of it has not survived, has decomposed, or has been lost. This fate may even extend to bits of evidence as modern as an alleged photograph of a dead Thunderbird, as will be discussed.

Birds that might have been Thunderbirds were vulnerable, according to the Indians who first knew them. Supposedly, they have been wounded, captured, and killed. Anthropologist Stanley Vestal related that Chief Hump of the Hunkpapa Dakota had captured one with "zigzag markings." [2] According to James Mooney, a Comanche hunter once wounded a large bird. Summoning help, the Comanche approached a ravine where the fallen bird was lying when thunder and lightning issued from the ravine. [3]

Mary Eastman, in the mid 19th century, recorded a Dakota oral tradition that "long ago" a Thunderbird had fallen from the sky and lay dead near Little Crow's village in Minnesota. [4] Gladwell Richardson was shown the rotting remains of a giant bird he had heard much about in Oklahoma. [5]

The "big eagle" (omaxsapitau) of the Blackfoot could be killed and its remains were examined. Also, they sometimes found this bird's nests, removed the young to raise them in captivity, and killed them at maturity. [6]

According to an informant of Claude Schaeffer, as late as the 1940s a wing of an extraordinary bird was "in the possession of a curio dealer in Calgary." [7] Another informant knew of even more remains existing in the same period. They were to be found ". . . among the Cree Indians of Hobbema, south of Edmonton. He had been told by a Cree from that place that the ceremonial regalia of a performer in the Grass Dance consisted of the stuffed body, wings, and tail of one of these birds." [8] These remains seem to have been of a size that they might also have originated from condors, as Schaeffer suggested. They would be of great interest whatever their origins.

The poor capacity of humankind to restrain something like a giant bird dictates that captured birds cannot be of great size. In Kentucky in 1870, the bird at Stanford had a wingspan of 7 feet (2.1 meters). [9] Around 1898, according to Robert Lyman's research, a bird turned up in Crawford County in Pennsylvania. A farmer set a trap and caught a large gray bird that was recalled to Lyman by Arch P. Akeley, who had seen it for himself. [10]

The Quinault Indians found a live whale still thrashing in the mountains and observed the gradual deterioration of its corpse. [11] Whales marked by talons have also been reported found in trees. [12] The loss of such prey presumably would be a rare occurrence, but reportedly it happens.

Nests of the Thunderbirds by all accounts are not elaborate and are most noteworthy for the grim feature of the bones of their victims. Changes over time have removed the caves of the Piasa, and the force of the elements would routinely erase exposed nests. Indians in the Pacific Northwest reported nests in the Olympic Mountains and retained from those sites bones of whales as charms. [13]

The absence of well-preserved, reliable, and accessible physical evidence for Thunderbirds to this point in time is the inevitable consequence of no organized effort to preserve it.

CHAPTER 12

The Alleged
Photographic Evidence

THE PROVERBIAL VALUE OF A PICTURE BEING WORTH A thousand words is not a reliable estimate when controversy occurs. Photographic evidence of controversial subject matter will always bring to mind the saying that "Photographs don't lie, but photographers do." Such doubts put a heavy burden on anyone coming forward with photographic material to make a persuasive case for acceptance. In the case of Thunderbirds, claims for photographic evidence in support of the birds have not been persuasive.

Motion film already exists that is said to show a Thunderbird in flight. During the many sightings made in 1977 in Illinois, one observer picked up the camera he always took with him when outdoors and he shot 100 feet [30 meters] of color film. This observer was "Texas John" Huffer, a man who had spent years as a combat photographer in the Marines and was a contributor to bass fishing magazines. On the morning of July 30, 1977, he was fishing on an inlet of Lake Shelbyville with his son, when they sighted two birds in a tree. Huffer blew his boat's horn, and the birds took off. In the boat, they followed the larger of the two birds, and it landed in a tree. He filmed the bird as it continued to move from tree to tree. The other bird wasn't seen again. As related in chapter 3, the film was dismissed as showing only turkey vultures.

In defense of his film, Huffer was quoted in the Champaign-Urbana *Courier* by Wally Haas as saying: "A turkey vulture has a red ring around its neck and my film clearly shows no red ring. The head and the legs are very much different from that of a turkey vulture. I've seen turkey vultures thousands of times." [1]

According to newspaper accounts, the film was shown on

WCIA-TV in Champaign and on a CBS national news broadcast. [2] Two outtakes from this film were published, one by the Tuscola *Journal* [3] and another by way of United Press International in the Chicago *Sun-Times*. [4] They show the dark shape of a bird in flight above leafy tree branches.

To date this film has contributed nothing to our knowledge of Thunderbirds. It has been dismissed as a film showing mere turkey vultures. The absence of a clear source of scale in the film has allowed this to happen. And the testimony of witnesses present has been simply ignored by those who don't want to accept it as evidence. Perhaps one day a more broad-minded consideration and careful scrutiny of this film will be productive. As an outdoorsman and cameraman with professional interests, Huffer kept his camera ready at all times, preparation that made him likely to obtain rare film such as this might be. As video cameras become more commonplace, other people may also catch rare footage of things seen in the outdoors but not readily believed. For them, as for Huffer, there will not exist any organized response to evaluate and preserve their footage.

If similar circumstances develop in the future, hopefully more could be done to provide a basis for assessing the value of the film. An independent record could be made of all witnesses, their statements, and significant events leading up to and following the filming. The scene of the event could be visited, filmed, and the film re-created with unquestionable objects of known scale to support what would otherwise be subjective guesswork. This evaluation should be done immediately following the event, before trees fall down, water levels rise or fall, and other changes occur in the environment. An independent record of the experience and of any physical evidence (such as the bird dung alleged by Huffer) would be valuable. Such efforts would require time, personnel, and equipment. These efforts cannot now be expected to take place for any future film event.

Other photographic evidence may also exist. In the early 1970s, a hopeful search developed for an alleged photograph, often described as a portrayal of a dead bird nailed to a wall. Before the wall stood six adult men lined up with arms outstretched fingertip to fingertip. The bird's wingspan was 36 feet (11 meters). Claims were made that this photo first appeared in a certain newspaper in the West in 1886 and also had been published in some recent magazine. The latter claim caused many people to say they remembered seeing it somewhere. The former claim had the modern editors of that Western newspaper denying that they had any record of such a photo. They have been mercilessly harassed by inquiries about it. The files of the paper have been searched repeatedly without success.

Two separate stories seem to have become entangled, causing much frustration all around. The first story is undoubtedly more than a century old. On April 26, 1890, the Tombstone *Epitaph* in the Arizona Territory printed a story about two ranchers meeting some large animal in the desert. [5] The original printing of this story in the *Epitaph* has been confirmed. In 1930, the story was reprinted by Horace Bell in his book *On the Old West Coast.* [6] Writer J. K. Parrish then used the same story in an article on "monsters" that appeared in the Fall 1969 issue of *Old West* magazine. [7]

Parrish's article prompted a letter from Harry F. McClure that contained some corroboration of the original story. He recalled details of it and had seen the two ranchers himself as a youth in Lordsburg, New Mexico, where the story was much discussed at that time. [8] Whatever the creature was, the *Epitaph* and McClure agreed that it was no bird. It didn't have a single feather. It appeared to be some kind of pterodactyl-like animal. [9] According to McClure, it was never captured, let alone killed, so it could not have been nailed to anybody's wall. No photograph was mentioned by anyone in relation to this particular account. In the course of 100 years this Arizona creature-story seems to have been incorrectly assumed to be the basis for that famous but seldom-seen photograph.

From the known record, the second story of a bird photograph goes back no further than 1963, when Jack Pearl told it in *Saga* magazine. [10] He wrote that in 1886, a photograph was published in the *Epitaph* that showed a huge bird nailed to a wall (whose wall or what kind of wall was not specified). Six men posed in the photo as described earlier in front of a 36-foot (11-meter) bird. Two prospectors were supposed to have killed the creature and brought it into Tombstone by wagon, according to Pearl.

The next person to write of this photo was Hiram M. Cranmer, resident of Hammersley Fork, Pennsylvania. In 1950, 1956, 1958, 1963, and 1966, *Fate* magazine received and published letters from Cranmer. [11] These letters were devoted wholly or in part to his views on Thunderbirds. He and others had seen them near his home. In this way, his name, address, and interest in the birds were widely circulated. Cranmer's first reference to photographs came in September 1963, when he wrote of two photographs. As he told it, the Tombstone story was moved to around 1900, and a second picture was supposed to show actors posing as professors with the bird nailed to the wall of the *Epitaph*. In the March 1966 *Fate* the story was further embellished and Cranmer noted that he had been getting mail from the magazine's readers. He credited "a lady in Tombstone, Ariz." for his account of the prospectors and the bird photographs.

The naturalist and fortean author Ivan T. Sanderson claimed to have possessed a photostatic copy of the six-men-with-bird photograph. He loaned it to two friends, Jay Blick and Frank Graves, who, sometime around 1966, took it into the Pennsylvania mountains, where they were looking into Thunderbirds. When the photostat wasn't returned and couldn't be found, Sanderson began searching for another copy. He discovered that many people responded that they recalled seeing it somewhere, but couldn't say exactly where. [12]

Many people have now written about this picture, but only Sanderson has published a claim to have possessed a copy for any length of time. He echoed Pearl's story of its origin, but he added one detail. The bird, he said, was nailed to a *barn* wall. This writer knew Sanderson at that time and never heard directly from him a clue as to where his photostat was obtained.

Hiram Cranmer made no claim to possess any photograph when writing to *Fate*, but others have said that he had a copy of a bird photo that was lost when his house burned down.

Much fruitless searching for a historically recent appearance of the photograph took place in the 1970s. Imprecise recollections caused speculation to shift from one popular publication to another. Among them was *Fate* magazine itself, but searching through decades of magazines brought no results. The editor of the Tombstone *Epitaph* pleaded in the letters column of *Fate* in 1966 that he had searched his files back 65 years and found nothing on the bird and no photographs. [13] An *Epitaph* editor in 1984 wrote in his own paper that Ben Traywick had thoroughly—but fruitlessly— searched for the bird story and photograph in Arizona and California newspapers of a century ago. [14]

Independently, a Canadian researcher sorted out the early and typically varied publishing record (mergers and name changes) of the *Epitaph*. But the photo was nowhere in the old files. The *Epitaph* does not have the answers to this puzzle and should be allowed to retire from any consideration.

On this topic I would like to make a few observations based on my personal knowledge of the search for the photo and of some of the people involved in the hunt.

The simple description of the photo—the six men posed to show the size of the dead bird—seems to create a vivid mental image in the minds of many, causing people who have always been particularly curious and eclectic in their knowledge to think it was somehow familiar even when they are unlikely to have ever seen it. Enough people have independently confessed to this reaction that I suspect it has contributed to the mistaken ideas about this photo. People may think they have seen it when they have not.

If the photograph does exist, it probably has nothing to do with the Tombstone paper. The photo probably was not widely published, as has been loosely asserted. The "barn wall" could just as well be in Kentucky or Pennsylvania as somewhere in the West. A credible story of its origin (subject to examination and, hopefully, verification) must accompany the photo if it is to have any value.

Serious consideration should be given to the possibility that a genuine photo does not exist. Sanderson may have been mistaken on this point. The photostatic reproduction he claimed to have might have been someone's hoax, or he might not have ever had anything more than a sketch showing the famous elements of the picture. For a long time, the only formal record of support for his ever having such a photostat was meager. In a letter to *Fate* for October 1974, a reader recalled seeing Sanderson appear with his photostat on a Pierre Berton television program in Canada sometime during 1963 to 1966. [15] John Keel has since added his recollection of seeing the picture in Sanderson's possession.

Consideration should also be given to the possible existence of a photograph—real or hoaxed—that was mistakenly entangled into the matter-of-record Arizona-creature story of 1890. Ivan Sanderson, as an author of many books and popular articles on mysteries, received a lot of mail from people who knew of his special interests. This writer can attest to this, having personally examined such mail. Hiram Cranmer claimed to have found many correspondents on Thunderbirds through *Fate*. Either—or both—of these men could have received a copy of an unusual photo from someone who had saved it for its uniqueness.

The photo might never have been published anywhere. And if it had been published, it might have appeared only once in one of America's many newspapers, in a book or booklet of local history, or in a popular magazine (in the last case, especially in the letters-to-the-editor column). Factually, almost nothing is known about this alleged photograph.

After the many years of fruitless searching by myself and others, there are few things to add to the topic. One thing to clarify is the quality of the alleged picture. Some people have overlooked the nature of the photostatic copy that has been cited here. These people have assumed that the picture allegedly lost was an 8 x 10 glossy picture that would have been treated as a "treasured heirloom." No one to my knowledge has claimed to have had such an item. By today's standards, photostats of the period involved were poor-quality copies, even when judged by the quality of copies 30 years ago. Photostats were made on thin paper and ill suited to reproduce photographs.

The clarity of the image may have been poor and any accompanying text may have been hard to read or illegible. I don't know if this was the case. This would be a case to have been made by the few people, such as Ivan Sanderson and John Keel, who have claimed to have held this picture. Unfortunately, they have never made a good presentation of what they saw, when they saw it, and where it came from. The time has passed for that to be done. (Naturally, I do not fault someone whose only chance to see it was on a television screen.)

The very subject matter of the alleged photo has been hedged by John Keel and stated by others to be something other than a bird. Keel has called it "the Thunderbird/pterodactyl photo." [16] I've also heard from people who tell me they have seen a picture of a pterodactyl-like creature. It was strung up behind people in Western garb; the photograph was an old sepia-toned photograph and appeared in a book of Western history or lore. It may be true that such a picture is the one remembered by everyone—or it may only be more confusion generated by the past 40 years of speculation on this subject.

What should bother everyone who hopes to see this picture is that those who have seen it keep coming up with different versions of it in their memories.

My own expectation at this point in time is that there is a picture of a large dead bird somewhere in an old book. I think that a small number of people have actually seen that particular record. I think that many other people are only responding to the description of that kind of a photograph and are confusing that description with some picture they have seen of a commonplace bird. If this is correct, then one day the right person will come upon that old record and share it with us.

I am also expecting that little or nothing of the story behind that photograph will be found in that old record. If the story of its origin has been preserved, I think we would have heard more of it, but we haven't been that lucky. So the uncovering of this photograph is likely to open up many questions that will need to be explored further.

The story from Arizona is simply about an entirely different kind of creature, but people seem to have a lot of trouble accepting this simple fact.

The status of the infamous "Thunderbird photograph" has remained the same for many years. A lot of people think they have seen the picture. Everyone wants to see it. But no one can produce a copy of it.

Before exploring the subject of giant fossil birds, we will consider that giant birds are not confined to North America. The same questions of truth behind legend are manifested worldwide, as we will see in the next chapter.

CHAPTER 13

Ancient Terrors
from the Skies

THUNDERBIRDS ARE PRESENTED AS A COMMON ITEM in mythologies around the world. An entry in *Everybody's Cyclopedia* for 1912 was typical in identifying the birds as "personifying thunder or its cause" among peoples in such diverse places as the Caribbean, Brazil, the Cook Islands in the Pacific, Burma (the Karens), and southern Africa (among the Bechuanas and the Basutos). [1] Does such an association necessarily mean that no such bird could exist? The Japanese regard the ptarmigan (Lagopus) that lives on mountaintops as sacred to the God of Thunder. They call this bird rai-cho, or "thunder bird." Pictures of it have been regarded by some Japanese farmers as a charm against lightning. [2]

A traditional view of Thunderbirds as a widely shared myth can be found in *The Life and Lore of the Bird* by Edward A. Armstrong. [3] In it appears evidence of the longevity of mankind's dealing with giant birds, whether they are real or imagined. Armstrong reproduced a pictograph of Neolithic age found in Turkey, which illustrated two headless figures confronted by a giant vulture-like bird. [4] Giant birds populate the continents of the world in legend and in tales told as true. Birds to reckon with were known in the ancient world and have been noted since on the continents of Africa, Asia, Europe, and South America. We will look at these traditions in this chapter before going on to look at giant fossil birds in the next chapter.

The classic example of the giant predatory bird has been the Roc (also Rukh, Ruc) of "Arabian Nights" fame. The tales of Sinbad's voyages told of his encounters with an enormous egg and the sky-darkening bird so large that it unknowingly carried Sinbad.

The bird could carry off the elephant and the rhinoceros and could sink ships by dropping boulders. The "giant feathers" taken to the Great Khan of Asia as evidence of the bird were probably fronds of the raffia palm. [5]

Among the earliest records of history are seals of ancient Sumeria showing the giant eagle Imgig, which could carry off the antelope. [6] Other ancient flying creatures known to share Roc-like characteristics were the Angka in Arabia; the Bar Yachre and the Ziz in Hebrew legends; the Chamrosh, the Eorosh, the Saena, and the Simurgh in Persia (Iran); the Garuda in Indonesia; and the Kargas in Turkey. Many of these are discussed by Ernest Ingersoll in chapter 10 of *Birds in Legend, Fable and Folklore* (1923) and by Joe Nigg in

Neolithic rock art found in Turkey. Redrawn by author from Edward A. Armstrong, The Life and Lore of the Bird *(NY: Crown, 1975).*

THUNDERBIRDS

The Roc of legend was said to carry off elephants. Drawing by the author, based on an image in Edward W. Lane, The Thousand and One Nights *(1859).*

A Guide to the Imaginary Birds of the World (1984). [7] The views they express range from all of the birds being completely imaginary creations to some suggested parallels with well-known birds. They exclude any physical reality in past and present for true giants.

Ancient Persia (what is now known as Iran) was home to several of these fierce birds. Just as the nearly forgotten Thunderbirds have surfaced unrecognized in modern times, so the Simurgh (or Imgig, or one of its relatives) may have turned up in modern Iran. In 1967, "two giant eagles" reportedly made an appearance over northwestern Iran. Notice of this was taken by James Clarke in *Man Is the Prey.* [8] In this event, two children, aged three and five, were picked up from the village of Jagelan. Both died when they were dropped from a height. Clarke disbelieved this report for the same reason the Lowes of Lawndale, Illinois, and other people have not found a receptive audience in modern times: no recognized bird could perform such a feat.

Perhaps such feats have taken place in the past in Persia, in the present in Iran, and in other parts of the world throughout time because an unrecognized species of giant birds has always been there, less obvious now than they once were, but holding out against extinction.

The Roc itself may have been inspired by—or had its legend sustained by—a genuine bird in Africa. In seeking such a bird, we can eliminate the elephant bird (*Aepyornis maximus*), despite the many suggestions that this heavy but flightless giant from Madagascar could be linked to the Roc. Since 1849, attempts have been made to equate this fossil bird with the Roc. [9] Its remarkable eggs, still found on its former island home, are wonderfully large. But to associate a grounded bird of any size with the mighty Roc is a dubious effort. Also, the albatross (*Diomedea exulans*) and the Cape vulture (*Gyps coprotheres*) of southern Africa, despite their long-standing nominations, hardly seem to have the menace to inspire a legend. [10]

Throughout southern Africa in the 15th century, the Portuguese heard of a black bird with the shape of an eagle but of a great size, too difficult to catch. [11] Further, a mapmaker in 1459 made note of a voyage that landed on the east coast of Africa about 1420. There the crew learned of the Chrocho, a formidable bird of prey with a name similar to the Roc but with a place in the historical record. [12] In fact, the people of the island of Madagascar long claimed to know of a giant bird of prey, but this point has always been discarded, owing to the presence of the elephant bird and its eggs. [13] But flightless birds can coexist with flying birds, as will be seen below in New Zealand.

The Roc of Africa that the Portuguese knew may have existed and fed not on the adults of African species, but on the young of the species, just as Thunderbirds of North America favored the immature individuals among their prey.

Certainly the Roc holds a firm place in fable with its eggs as big as a house and its image of two doomed elephants in its talons and a third in its mighty beak. A more modest but still gigantic bird may have inspired or sustained this venerable fable.

In the 20th century, scattered about sub-Saharan Africa are hints that a modern Roc might still survive there. But, first of all, notice should be taken here that on the Dark Continent, as elsewhere in the world, there are reports of black flying creatures resembling the ancient pterodactyl and even very large bats. [14] As recently as the summer of 1988, a giant pterodactyl was reported from Namibia (formerly Southwest Africa). [15] Throughout this book, I've tried to present evidence and consideration specifically on large flying birds and to avoid lengthy digressions into other topics.

In 1928, G.W.B. Huntingford found among the Nyala in East Africa a fear of being carried off at night. They feared "a kind of evil spirit which appears at night and takes the form of a black bird." [16] In the Congo in 1980, biologist Roy Mackal, who is known for his willingness to pursue unusual animals, talked to a political officer, Andre Monelle. This man had seen an unusual bird that was known to live in the jungle. Its wingspan reached 13 feet (4 meters) and its numbers seemed to be declining. [17] The same bird, further to the east, may have been noted briefly by Attilio Gatti in *The Great Mother Forest*. The pygmies of the Ituri Forest told him of "a bird so enormous and powerful that it could reduce to a pulp the strongest man." [18]

Finally, in 1903 in Rhodesia (now Zimbabwe), George H. France observed his giant bird in flight and, typically, the bird also rested in a tree. Discussion of the American Thunderbirds prompted him to write from Windsor, Ontario, to *Fate* magazine in 1964. [19]

Giant birds were known across southern Asia as well. The Garuda was known as an ancient and powerful being, half-man and half-bird. [20] In Malaya it was a bird, the Gerda. Malay peasants also knew a "fabulous vulture," the *Jintayu* (identified as *Jatayu* in Sanskrit). [21] The Garuda in Indonesia was a giant bird that preyed on human beings. [22] Birds carrying off people were known among the Tinguian in the Philippines as well. [23]

The limits of size among known birds are not always certain, raising questions of what giant birds might be seen. An example of oversized eagles took place in 1968 off the southeast coast of Tasmania, at Bruny Island. Two wedge-tailed eagles (*Aquila audax*) with wingspans of 11 feet (3.3 meters) were seen by a farmer to carry off two lambs. [24] Leslie Brown in *Eagles of the World* wrote that individuals of this species spanning more than 10 feet (3 meters) were doubtful, exceeding the accepted limit by 2 feet (60 cm). [25]

In New Zealand, a large eagle known only from fossils, *Harpagornis*, has been linked with a Maori tradition of a bird called the Hokioi since the 1870s. [26] This association seems to have become generally accepted. *Harpagornis* was a large eagle capable of feasting on the largest of the moas, the famous flightless birds of New Zealand. It did so when the moas were mired in swamps. [27]

The Maoris had another name for a large bird, this one a man-eating bird. Many tales were told of the Pou-kai (also Poua-kai). [28] and there is an area called the Pouakai Mountains on the North Island of New Zealand. [29] A legend of a South Island tribe, the Waitaha, told of the habits of the Pou-kai. This bird "had its nests on the spur of a mountain, called Tawera, from where it darted down, seizing and carrying off men, women, and children as food for itself and its young." The bird took its prey so quickly that no one escaped it. Johannes Anderson wrote in *Myths and Legends of the Polynesians* that "its wings made a loud noise as it flew through the air." [30] On the island of Fiji, the Ngani-vatu (or Ngutu-lei) was a giant man-eating bird. [31]

From the ancient world in southern Europe, giant birds figured in the sixth labor of Hercules. The birds of the Styphalides, stork-like and as large as cranes, were devourers of men when found in northern Arcadia in Greece. According to Pausanias, a Greek traveler of the fifth century, the birds originally came from Arabia. [32]

In modern Europe, Cornwall in the south of England was the source of unusual bird reports in 1976 and 1978. According to the accounts, this creature would have to be a European cousin of the giant owls appearing in North America. With a better descriptive flair, the animal was dubbed "Owlman." Drawings by witnesses show a large winged creature as big as a man. [33]

Another mystery popped up a few years later that sounds a lot more like a European relative of the Thunderbirds. The sightings popped up in the neighborhood of Bradford along the Pennine Mountains that stretch north to south in the middle of England.

The story was recalled in 2003 and billed as "the Big Bird riddle that was never solved." Journalist Mike Priestley of the Bradford *Telegraph & Argus* had pursued reports of a Big Bird over and near North Bradford in 1982 and 1983. He chased it for three weeks and was able to take a photograph of it. He saw it circling several times at a great distance, and only once did it circle down into range. The picture showed the outline of an eagle-like bird of prey with the near-headless appearance that goes with a bare head and neck. [34]

Europe has been the scene of several birds reported to carry off children and other objects with weights considered to exceed the ability of known birds. Felix Pouchet related in *The Universe* the case of Marie Delex from the Swiss canton of Valais in 1838. This five-year-old girl was snatched by an eagle from in front of a playmate. Two months later, her corpse was found on a mountain ledge by a shepherd. [35]

In *Living Wonders*, John Michell and Robert J. M. Rickard gave some details of incidents reported over many years of birds carrying off human babies in such places as Scotland, Switzerland, Italy, Syria, and Turkey. [36]

A well-researched incident in Norway in 1932 may contribute to understanding these events and to providing valuable perspective whenever a similar event is considered. In this incident, a young girl in Norway was reported to have been carried off by a Gray sea eagle (*Haliaetus albicilla*) and dropped on a mountain ledge. This story was brought to the attention of the English-speaking world 30 years later by Doug Storer. [37] Roger Caras commented on it in the first edition of his book *Dangerous to Man*. In the second edition, it wasn't mentioned. [38] Gerald Wood included this report in the third edition of the *Guinness Book of Animal Facts and Feats*. [39]

An entire Norwegian-language book about this event appeared in 1960. Called *Eagle's Prey*, it was also published in Swedish and Icelandic, but not in English. Sixteen years later, the author, Steiner Hunnestad, was still defending his authentication of the event when he wrote an article for Oslo's *Aftenposten* for January 21, 1976. I have had that article translated especially to provide information—such as the child's weight—not given in the brief English-language treatments cited above.

In Norway on June 5, 1932, when Svanhild Hansen was three years old (an age of four years appeared in Storer) a Gray sea eagle carried her 1.2 miles (2 kilometers). An investigation showed that that she was taken from the Kvaloyvik bogs to Haga Mountain on the island of Leka. Her passage was not witnessed, but after a search for seven hours she was found alive on a shelf of rock 65 feet (20 meters) below an eagle's nest. The child was examined and weighed by Dr. K. Fossum, a district physician. She weighed 42 pounds (19 kilograms).

While no one witnessed the flight, nearly 100 people were involved in the search and testified to the facts. The bog and mountain terrain required the child to have been flown to the spot where she was found. A zoologist, Dr. Hartvig Huitfeldt-Kaas, spent a month on Leka in 1932 researching the event and found it to be "completely reliable."

The bird responsible for the flight was later seen to fly always with its legs hanging down, apparently stretched by the experience. Some called it the "Svanhild-eagle." [40]

When "giant birds" are said to spirit away large children and bigger animals with ease, then a case is being made for truly unrecognized birds. But the experience at Leka Island in Norway is evidence that the mere lifting of a child of even 42 pounds (19 kilograms) alone is not always a definite indicator of such unusual birds. Mountainous conditions could assist known birds in lifting an out-of-the-ordinary burden. If the sea eagle can perform as indicated in Norway, other large birds of prey may be responsible for similar achievements.

Northern Europe has numerous ancient wonder birds to its credit. In the 16th century, Olaus Magnus, a Swedish ecclesiastic and historian, identified Griffons as birds living in the mountains and preying on both humans and horses. [41] To Laplanders, the Vuokho was another giant bird with an evil reputation. [42]

Until 1991 in the U.S., the only modern report hinting of such birds that was known was one from Sweden. In the woods near Kristianstad a sighting of a giant black bird took place on May 21, 1973. [43]

In October of 1991 a report from northern Norway suggested that formidable predatory birds were doing well in that part of the globe. The news was extracted from a Norwegian newspaper by Steve Newman, who has been putting together a syndicated weekly column called "Earthweek" which covers environmental issues. In October 1991, a column included this report:

> Lapp herders in northern Norway claim that huge eagles ate about 1,300 of their reindeer this year, and are demanding compensation from the government. The Oslo tabloid *Dagbladet* reported that officially only five eagles have been reported in the entire country, and suggested that if the eagles are as large as the herders claim, "they're going to have to start using an airport when they come in for a landing." Odd Ronningen, an environmental official, admitted that some herders exaggerate, but said that wild animals killed 25,000 of their reindeer in 1989. [44]

As with the Thunderbirds in North America, when the Griffon/Vuokho is reported in today's world, it's ignored.

The *Dictionary of Fabulous Beasts* by Richard Barber and Anne Riches noted that the Kreutzet in ancient Muscovy exceeded the eagle in size and was a terror to other birds. The inhabitants of Poland knew the same bird as Bialozar. [45] The Vikhar (Vikhor) was a Slavic god of the whirlwind characterized as a giant eagle. [46]

In eastern Asia, the Chukchees inhabiting Siberia knew the Nogabird, which added elk and whales to its diet of people. [47] The Noga was probably the same as the Norka appearing in Russian fiction. [48] The Thunderbirds appear again full blown and designated with that same name in northern Siberia, according to Uno Holmberg in volume 4 of *Mythology of All Races*. The Forest Tungus, the Yakuts, the Chukchees, the Samoyeds, and the Ostiaks all knew this bird. [49]

Thunderbirds have appeared not only in northern Asia and North America but also in parts of South America. The West Indies and Central America, geographically part of North America, also have contributed to bird lore in the New World.

In South America, we encounter the presence of the Andean condor (*Vultur gryphus*) and again the possible confusion of this bird with something much larger. The impressive condor reaches a wingspan of 12 feet (3.7 meters), but more generally its wingspan is 10 feet (3 meters). An adult weighs 26 to 35 pounds (11.8 to 16 kilograms). They range from Colombia to Tierra del Fuego, the length of the continent, according to Colin Pennycuick, an ornithologist at the University of Miami who has studied the birds in the wild. [50]

The earliest Spanish reports of the Andean condor compared them to the Roc, according to Philip Henry Gosse. The bird was said to attack men and carry off stags. [51] Later observations of the condors found them to be less offensive.

The size of the Andean condor is a point on which a few writers have stumbled, having the misfortune to have quoted an early traveler, Edmond Temple, whose *Travels in Various Parts of Peru* was published in 1835. On page 415 of volume 2 appeared a passage that he advised was "taken down with my own hand" and that claimed to measure the wingspan of a dead bird as 40 feet (12 meters). The passage followed his telling of his slaying of an Andean condor. But two pages later, Temple wrote that he had only played a trick on his readers by inserting a quotation from *The Travels of Marco Polo*. [52]

The victims of this trick who cited Temple's claim while unaware of the later correction have included:

- Philip Henry Gosse in *Romance of Natural History* (1861) [53]
- Rev. H.C. Adams in an otherwise delightful book, *Travellers' Tales* (1882) [54]
- Gerald Wood, as recently as 1972, in the first edition of *Animal Facts and Feats*. [55] It didn't appear in later editions.

Not all readers were victims. Henry Yule, in his extensive commentaries on Marco Polo's travels, correctly noted Temple's jest. [56]

Tony Morrison, in *Land Above the Clouds*, sketched the Andean condor's habits, and then wrote that Indians in the mountains "have tales of giant birds that sweep down from the heavens and snatch lambs from the flock before soaring again to the mountain tops." They accused the Andean condor of taking llamas and sheep when very young. He cited two reports he heard, one from a helicopter pilot and one from a mining engineer. They had seen condors carrying off small animals. Morrison had never seen a condor carry anything. He suggested the witnesses might be mistaking the Black-chested hawk (*Buteo fuscescens*) for the condor. [57]

Thunderbirds have been catalogued among the beliefs of South American Indians by professional anthropologists as well. The birds were known in the foothills of the Andes among the

A "vulture devouring man" from a sculpture in Guatemala. The original artwork has been lost. Reprinted from Herman Streibel, "The Sculptures of Santa Lucia Cozumahualpa, Guatemala, in the Hamburg Ethnological Museum," Smithsonian Institution, Annual Report for 1899 (Washington: GPO, 1901).

Chiriguano and in the Gran Chaco among the Mataco, Lengua, Ashluslay, Choroti, and Chane. Elsewhere, they were found on the coast of Brazil with Cariri and in the northwest of Brazil with Caaxinaua (Cashinawa). On the coast of Ecuador the belief appeared among the Cayapa.

THUNDERBIRDS

In the Guianas and the West Indies, Thunderbirds were known among the Caribs and the Wapisiana (Wapishiana). [58]

The modern world of the Caribbean still may be haunted by the Thunderbirds of old. The skies over the district of Moca, Puerto Rico, were visited by some large bird. In March 1975, people repeatedly reported a gray or "whitish" bird with a long neck flying about. One man reported that it attacked him. Small domesticated animals were killed. A "loud screech" and the sound of flapping wings sometimes accompanied the deaths. [59]

Another report occurred as recently as 1991. Birds were reported by Cruz Fidalgo and others who were out shrimp fishing. They were on a river flowing out of the Yunque Mountains when they spied "this great huge thing, like a big bird. . . . It looked like an eagle with very beautiful golden feathers." Another bird like the first flew by later. [60]

An ancient sculpture from Central America embodies the mystery that the past offers up to the present. In Guatemala at Santa Lucia Cozumahualpa, an image in stone more than a thousand years old was recorded in a drawing made in 1862. (The sculpture itself was later lost when it was dropped in the ocean while being moved.) Described as a "vulture-devouring man," this work depicted a man in the beak of a giant bird. Commenting on the picture, Herman Strebel identified the bird as the King Vulture (*Sarcoramphus papa*) but acknowledged that this representation wasn't in line with the usual functions of that bird in the cultures of the area. [61]

Here is another picture akin to the pictograph of Turkey, clearly showing the gigantic man-devouring vulture-like birds found in worldwide traditions. Do we correctly interpret them when we deny the possibility that they could be mankind's record of true birds? Such birds could have existed long ago, known as Imgig, as Vuokho, as Thunderbird, or by many names both known and forgotten. And they could survive today, few in number and rarely acknowledged by a world that never wanted to confront them.

CHAPTER 14

Wonder Birds

THE PREVIOUS CHAPTERS SUGGEST THAT GIGANTIC birds have survived from earlier times by virtue of their adaptability, mobility, and reduced visibility to the present occupants of North America. If this proposition is correct, there is little doubt about the ornithological identity of the predatory hawk-like Thunderbirds. Fossil finds known since 1952 have demonstrated the past existence of such a formidable creature. Similar birds might survive in the Americas and around the world.

The fossil genus of birds *Teratornis* has been linked with the legend of Thunderbirds for more than 55 years. ("Teratorn" means "wonder bird" in Greek.) In 1948, Osmond P. Breland, a zoologist at the University of Texas, wrote briefly in *Animal Facts and Fallacies* about Thunderbirds being known among the North American Indians. He then noted "the recent discovery in California of the remains of an enormous eaglelike bird" in fossil form. The skull and other bones indicated a bird two times the size of a bald eagle. Breland made clear his doubt that this bird could ever have killed bison or flown off with people as described in legends. He concluded: "It thus seems quite possible that the thunderbird legend of the western Indians was based upon a bird that actually did exist at one time and it may be that the bird also attacked human beings." [1]

In 1963, Breland's book and another of his were combined into *Animal Life and Lore*. There he retained the identical statement on Thunderbirds, dropping only the word "recent" before "discovery." [2] Breland didn't specify which fossil bird he meant, but he could only have been referring to Merriam's teratorn (*Teratornis merriami*). Early finds indicated a bird with a wingspan of about 12 feet (3.6 meters). Its wingspan is now known to have reached 14 feet (4.2 meters). They were predatory, ground-stalking birds. Many of them became mired with their prey in the asphalt at Rancho La Brea in southern California. [3] This teratorn is also known from Mexico and Florida. [4] If the current view of its stalking habits is correct, this bird was indeed unlikely to have carried off people and larger prey.

Only in 1952 did a larger teratorn, *Teratornis incredibilis*, come to light from Nevada. Hildegarde Howard went through mammal bones from Smith Creek Cave that were collected in 1934 and 1936. Among them she found a large carpal bone from a raptor, one so large that it had been mistakenly left behind when the bird bones were sorted out. This find required the establishment of a new species. [5] The hypothetical wingspan of this bird was 17 feet (5.2 meters). [6]

In 1963, Englishman John Wakefield in *The Strange World of Birds* briefly treated the Thunderbirds as a symbol among the American Indians. On its identity his statements so paralleled those of Breland, referring to California birds and to the size of the bird, that he was clearly only echoing Breland's observations on Merriam's teratorn. [7]

In his 1963 *Saga* article, Jack Pearl credited R. J. Young, a California ornithologist, with putting forth the California condor as the Thunderbird. Young specifically cited larger specimens of this well-known bird as his candidate. The taking of live prey, otherwise unknown for condors, was attributed by Young to desperation from hunger. [8]

The first known effort to link Thunderbirds with *Teratornis incredibilis* came in 1964 in *Birds of Prey of the World* by Mary Louise Grossman and John H. Hamlet. They summarized the *T. merriami* and *T. incredibilis* finds and noted the existence of the Thunderbird as a symbol from Mexico to Alaska. They included a reference to a Blackfoot legend that could only be Claude Schaeffer's Omaxsapitau. The fossils and the legends indicated to them "a wide range for the big condors on the North American continent within the memory of man." [9]

In 1969, Theodore Downs of the Natural History Museum

of Los Angeles County announced more finds of *T. incredibilis* from the Anza-Borrego Desert in southern California. The wingspan was thought to be 18 feet (5.5 meters). [10] The bird was 40 percent larger than the Rancho La Brea teratorns. Hildegarde Howard published these finds in *Condor* in 1972. [11]

Publicity in 1969 for the latest fossil finds sparked my greater interest in the Thunderbird legends. That publicity may also have been responsible for the renewed search for the alleged wall photograph discussed in chapter 12.

From this point on, in the 1970s considerations of the Thunderbirds among forteans commonly included references to the teratorns, as evidenced in the Res Bureau Bulletin in 1976. [12]

From Argentina in 1980 came news of a still larger find in the family of Teratornithidae. [13] Eduardo P. Tonni and Rosendo Pascual of the La Plata Museum had found fossils at a site 100 miles (161 kilometers) west of Buenos Aires. This bird was so large that when describing it the scientists had to argue that its flying ability required a revised understanding of avian flight.

Kenneth Campbell Jr. of the Natural History Museum of Los Angeles County examined the fossils and assisted in announcing the discovery. Estimates of the weight of *Argentavis magnificens* have ranged from 174 pounds (80 kilograms) to 265 pounds (120 kilograms). [14] On a wingspan of perhaps 25 feet (7.6 meters) the predatory "Magnificent Argentine Bird" glided and also flew with flapping flight. With the age of the fossils estimated as late Miocene, five to eight million years ago, this bird is not recognized as a recent inhabitant of the South American continent. Descendants of this bird clearly are candidates to explain Thunderbirds in both North and South America.

The find of another large teratorn, *Aiolornis incredibilis*, has been made near Murrieta, in Riverside County, California. "The Incredible Bird of the Winds" is thought to have had a wingspan of 18 feet (5.5 meters). Ornithologists like to think that these large birds stalked their prey on the ground. [15]

After Jack Pearl in 1963 and Robert Lyman in 1973, the third writer to pen anything at length on Thunderbirds as real birds was fortean researcher Loren Coleman in 1985. A chapter in his *Curious Encounters* brought together modern accounts of the birds and cited the giant teratorns as the likely source of them. [16]

Thunderbirds are not the California condor (*Gymnogyps californianus*), but the fate of this bird may be instructive to the future of Thunderbirds. Writers have frequently expressed the natural assumption that the condor in the American West was the subject of mythic associations for the American Indians, producing a Thunderbird of exaggeration. As earlier references to the condor have tried to indicate, in size, in habits, and in its range the condor cannot fill the bill as an inspiration for the mighty Thunderbirds and other giant birds across North America. The bird's size is modest; its diet is carrion; and its feet are incapable of grasping its food to be carried any noteworthy height or distance. This grand bird has dwindled in numbers in recent years to the point where it was nearly considered extinct in the wild in North America. In 1987, the last wild bird was taken into captivity in southern California. At that time the total number of birds in captivity in the state was 27. [17] Efforts are now underway to reintroduce the condors into the wild in California. The birds have been introduced into Arizona and Utah as well. [18]

The condor's known range in historic times was determined by Carl Koford in *The California Condor* in 1953. Koford considered the bird to have been confined to the Pacific coastal states from the lower Columbia River in Oregon down through California into northern parts of Baja California. He considered reports from Arizona to be doubtful. [19]

Other writers cited infrequent reports beyond Koford's limits for historic times. James Greenway Jr. allowed the bird's appearance in Arizona and mentioned a questionable report from Utah. [20] Arthur C. Bent had condors appearing as far north as Vancouver Island in British Columbia. [21] Claude Schaeffer argued for their appearance in Montana and Alberta during the 1800s. [22]

The accepted range of the condor in prehistory was called into question in 1987. As Koford's study indicated, in the Pleistocene condors were present in Mexico, Florida, and California. Later fossil finds predating historic records indicated the birds inhabited an area from Oregon to California and as far east as Brewster County, Texas. [23] In March 1987 came the announcement of a find of three fossilized condor bones in Genessee County, near Rochester, New York. They were 11,000 years old. [24] The condors may have been present throughout the United States when the large species of Pleistocène fauna provided a food source. [25]

Koford indicated that condors had disappeared from Lower California (the Baja) after being reported there from 1887 to 1937. [26] Later claims of sightings were pursued during five visits to Mexico from 1971 to 1979 by ornithologists Sanford R. Wilbur and Lloyd F. Kiff. According to *Oryx* for May 1981, they considered the claims to be caused by other birds of prey that were misidentified. *Oryx* reported further: "The very small amount of suitable habitat is regularly visited by ornithologists, who would certainly have seen any birds that had survived. . . ." [27]

Nevertheless, condors continue to be reported in the mountains around Valle de Trinidad in the Baja of Mexico. As an example, in the spring of 1987 Rosaldo Lopez Renterria, a pastor from Lazaro Cardenas, wrote to Bill Torre at the San Diego Wild Animal Park. He gave an accurate description of condors in telling of birds seen feeding on dead cows. Ornithologists do not accept such reports as accurate. [28] If their judgment is in error, the best hope for wild California condors lies in the remoteness and obscurity of a home in Mexico.

Humankind's inability to allow the condor the freewheeling living space it required is a sobering practical experience. Such living space is what giant birds would require, wherever they might be recognized in the future. Despite a long acquaintance with the threat to the condor and its needs, the bird has suffered—officially, at least—the disappearance of its natural identity as a wild creature.

The potential for overlooked giant birds can be found in places around the world. New Zealand is an example. We may eventually find a parallel situation to the American experience with fossil birds. First, Merriam's teratorn was found mired in great numbers with its prey at Rancho La Brea. Then, the larger teratorns were found elsewhere. *Harpagornis* has likewise been found mired where it fed. Maybe a larger form of this bird, known in Maori legend as Poua-kai, will yet be found in fossil form or even in living form as the Maoris claim to have known it.

In Africa a fossil form from the Eocene (34 to 58 million years ago) is the only evidence so far of *Gigantornis eaglesomei*, a bird with an estimated 25-foot (6-meter) wingspan. [29] This breastbone from Nigeria might be evidence of a bird that inspired the very Roc of legend.

The fossil record has giant birds of a size that can be the foundation for living giants. When some physical evidence of the living wonder birds is obtained and preserved, they will have ancestors.

CHAPTER 15

Bighoot

A SPECIES OF GIANT OWL, WHICH I'VE DUBBED "Bighoot," has been making appearances in West Virginia and the Ozarks. Another giant bird of prey that appears to have been overlooked, it would have survived for reasons similar to those that helped the Thunderbirds persist. Bighoot appears to be a capable predator, active largely at night, and able to fit into the modern environment by a means of camouflage known for owls. There is a record of such a creature in American Indian folklore. It has a predecessor in the fossil record of birds, and there are hints that it is not unique to North America.

This owl probably remains little known by being both rare and active almost exclusively at night. Owls make no nests and are adapted to silent flight. This bird would have characteristics similar to Thunderbirds in mobility and adaptability that permit the survival of a formidable predator. It would feed on small mammals and be menacing enough to threaten human beings. But people wouldn't need to be a regular part of the bird's diet.

A likely candidate would be a giant eagle owl still unrecognized by science as a modern bird. It would be related to the genus *Bubo*. Its closest relative would be the great horned owl in North America, which is identified by Michael Fogden as the New World representative of the eagle owl family. [1]

The abundance of nature has room for many creatures. The record of hardened bones we call fossils attests to this. We are slowly recording the past that has been captured by chance in circumstances where portions of animals have been fossilized, and there is no certainty that the record we can recover will be complete. The gaps that exist now might remain unfilled for all time. Fortunately for Bighoot, there's one fossil candidate just off the American shores.

Bighoot the giant owl can be several feet tall with a reported wingspan twice its height. With furled wings the owl can resemble a tree. (Art by Mark Rollins.)

THUNDERBIRDS

There is a large fossil owl known to have survived in Cuba until a few thousands of years ago, *Ornimegalonyx oteroi.* [2] It was as much as 3.3 feet [1 meter] tall. Its extinction date is reckoned to be 8,000 to 10,000 years ago. The fossil remains have been found in many caves in Cuba. It is thought to have roosted in caves and hunted in forests nearby for its prey, rodents and mammals.

This bird was at first thought to have been flightless, and therefore was given the name of Giant Cursorial Owl, i.e., a running owl. More complete skeletal remains then led to a consideration that this owl was capable of flying short distances. It is also known as *Buho gigante* in Spanish. So this owl was a large bird of prey but it was not, based upon the fossils presently known, a powerful flyer.

Typical of such "monsters," the American Indians knew Bighoot. The Passamaquoddy Indians in Maine had a name for it. A priest who ministered to these people, Father O'Dowd, observed that: "'Gee-bel-lowk' is otherwise known as the 'spirit of the night air.' Many Passamaquoddies gravely tell you that they have seen him, and that he is all legs and head, having no visible body. He is seen perching in the crotch of a tree, making ugly grins at whoever looks at him." [3]

To Indians such as the Iroquois, the Wyandot, and the Tuscarora, Bighoot was known as the "Flying Head," "Big Head," or "Great Head." It was portrayed by Richard Carylon in *A Guide to the Gods* this way: "Demonic deities of the Iroquois Indians. They were huge, bodiless heads covered in long hair from which protruded sharpnailed claws. With open mouths and fiery eyes the Big Heads flew about in storms, the wind keeping them up by their masses of hair." [4]

Another source for stories of the Iroquois, Erminnie Smith, gave this description of them: "It was a common belief among Indians that there was a strange, human-like creature, consisting simply of a head made terrific by large eyes and covered with long hair. His home was upon a huge rock, a rifted promontory, over which his long hair streamed in shaggy fierceness." [5]

The hair and fiery eyes of the "Flying Head" could have been the feathers of a bird and the red eye-shine that is characteristic of owls.

The Wyandot Indians, native to Ohio, identified this creature as carrying off their offspring, as noted by William Connelly: "The Flying Heads plagued the Wyandots. They were more dangerous and troublesome during rainy, foggy, or misty weather. They could enter a cloud of fog, or mist, or rain, and in it approach a Wyandot village unseen. They were wicked and cruel hooh-kehs and cannibals. They caused sickness, were vampires, and lay in wait for people, whom they caught and devoured. They carried away children; they blighted the tobacco and other crops; they stole and devoured the game after the hunter had killed it. Fire was the most potent agency with which to resist them. The lightning sometimes killed one." [6]

Across the continent the Apache Indians knew a creature they called Big Owl. Also, in Washington State, giant owls were said to be a menace to children. Along the Columbia River they were used to frighten children: "Spine-chilling tales were told to naughty children by the Wishram Indians of Washington about the old she-owl who snatched children away, and many other Indian peoples would warn children that if they did not behave they would be taken away by the owl—much the same as European children are frightened with the witch." [7]

In the middle of the continent Bighoot was known to the Omahas and the Ponkas. Folklorist James Owen Dorsey gave us this record: "In-da-dhin-ga. This is a monster in human shape according to the Omahas, but the Ponkas compare it to the great owl; saying that it is of huge size, and dwells in the forest, being able to pull up large trees by the roots. Mothers scare their children by saying, 'Take care, the Indadhinga will get you.'" [8]

The lore of the Shoshoni Indians in the American West included an owl said to carry off men for food. [9] The Hohoq (also Hoh-hok), which Joseph Wherry identified as a "spirit bird of the mountains" in the Pacific Northwest, may be the giant owl's parallel in symbolism to the Thunderbird in that area. [10]

The pioneers into the New World called this creature the "Booger Owl," as was noted in the Ozarks. [11]

In the 20th century, Bighoot became known as the Birdman when it was reported flying up and down the creeks of West Virginia. [12] We know of this due to the work of James Gay Jones, an emeritus professor of history at Glenville State College in West Virginia. He collected the folklore of his state in his books, including *Appalachian Ghost Stories* and *More Appalachian Ghost Stories*. In *Haunted Valley and More Folk Tales of Appalachia* he gave this account of Birdman in 1979.

> . . . . on a number of occasions since the early
> years of this century, a large bird with the head of
> a man and wingspread of at least a dozen feet [3.6
> meters], has been seen just prior to or immediate-
> ly after, a tragic occurrence at Point Pleasant
> [West Virginia]. Sightings of the birdman have
> been reported by a number of rural farm families
> in Mason, Jackson, Roane, Clay, and Kanawha
> counties. About the time of World War I, the bird-
> man was reported having been observed flying
> over the hamlet of Looneyville, up Johnson Creek
> and down Gabe in Roane County thence down
> the Elk Valley into the Kanawha. Its monstrous
> size and dark reddish feathers, which glistened in
> the sunlight, cast fear in all who saw it. Parents
> were so alarmed at its appearance that, for days
> afterward, they forebade their small children to
> play outside the house.

Jones went on to note that after World War II, people reported being pursued in their cars while driving near the Ohio River. Specifically this happened in Mason, Jackson, and Wood counties. Again we can observe that giant birds of prey have taken advantage of the modern automobile and the current of moving air it creates to assist them in flight.

Sadly, sightings in Ohio and West Virginia of Bighoot were tagged with the name of "Mothman" in 1966-67. They were reported upon by Helen M. White in *Fate* [13] and extensively by journalist John Keel. Keel's efforts to search out all odd reports, claims, and associated happenings in the area for that period resulted in articles in *Saga* for October 1968 and in *Flying Saucer Review* for July-August 1968. [14] He also incorporated this material into two of his books, *Strange Creatures from Time and Space* and *The Mothman Prophecies*. [15] Keel's analysis of his own work led him to consider that "Mothman" and UFOs also reported locally could have been related. This early stamp of being something from outer space has influenced most of the discussions of the reports since that time.

People were encountering Bighoot in southern Ohio and nearby parts of West Virginia in the mid-1960s. Here is a chronology of some of the events based upon the work of Helen White [16] and newspaper accounts at that time.

November 12, 1966: Kenneth Duncan saw something like a brown human being gliding through the trees at Reamer, West Virginia, near Clendenin (Kanawha County).

November 15, 1966: Two couples, the Mallettes and the Scarberrys, said they were pursued by large bird flying 50 feet [15.2 meters] over their car outside Pt. Pleasant. The thing was 6 feet [1.8 meters] tall, had red eyes, and looked like a man with wings.

November 25, 1966: Thomas Ury of Clarksburg saw something north of Pt. Pleasant. It rose from a field, flew over his car, and went off toward the Ohio River. It was 6 feet [1.8 meters] tall with a 10-foot [3-meter] wingspan.

November 26, 1966: A farmer, Marvin Shock, his family, and Ewing Tilton watched some birds in trees on Cat Creek outside Lowell, Ohio. Four large birds were seen. They had dark brown backs and gray breasts.

November 27, 1966: Connie Jo Carpenter said a man-like thing with a big wingspan flew toward her car near New Haven, West Virginia.

November 27, 1966: South of Pt. Pleasant at St. Albans, two young girls said they saw a big bird with red pop-eyes.

December 7, 1966: In Ohio, near the Athens and Hocking county line, four women from Nelsonville had a near-collision with a bird.

December 11, 1966: Near Wilson Straight, West Virginia, Kathryn Beaver of Leon said a flying creature glided toward her car. The impact on her was like a gust of wind.

More was learned about the incidents from renewed attention in 2001-2002. Publicity for the months of reports in the 1960s was generated by a new movie, *The Mothman Prophecies*. The

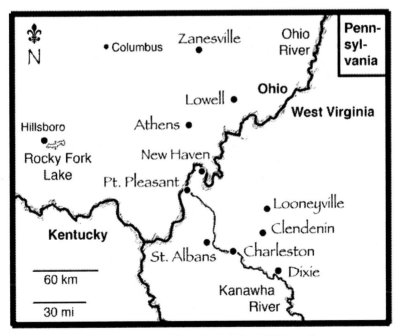

Southern Ohio and nearby parts of West Virginia are Bighoot Country. (Art by Mark Rollins.)

THUNDERBIRDS

movie was a psychological thriller about the possibility of prophecy taking place prior to a disaster. The figure of "Mothman" barely played a part in the film. For what it wanted to be, which is the way to judge a film, it does a good job, but it doesn't reflect in any way the creatures behind the reports that were made in the 1960s.

One person came forth with a story to tell about killing a giant owl at the time of the Mothman excitement decades ago. The look back at the whole experience caused one local resident in West Virginia to speak up.

Betty Sturgeon told her story to Bob Withers of the Huntington, West Virginia, *Herald-Disptach* in January of 2002:

> Betty Sturgeon of Ashton, W.Va., says her now-deceased husband, Calvin "Pood" Sturgeon, shot the creature and buried it near their mobile home on Eighteen Mile Creek Road.
>
> "He had seen it flying around, and we lost a dog about that time," Sturgeon says. "My husband would get up with a gun and go outside at night looking for it."
>
> One night, Sturgeon heard gunfire and heard her husband call, "Come out here."
>
> She recalls glancing at some kind of big bird, but she got scared and ran back in the house. "They had said not to shoot it," she says, referring to authorities' warnings that federal and state wildlife laws prohibit killing migratory birds of all kinds. "It was protected."
>
> Sturgeon says a new house was built in 1979 over the spot where her husband buried the creature. He died in 1996. [17]

Fear of the legal consequences for killing some odd animal comes up periodically in the history of cryptozoology, just as it has here in West Virginia. There is no one to counsel people and stand by them legally should they kill some protected species. So they take the course of action as described here that will protect them from legal entanglements. This is another practical reason that the dead bodies of strange animals are not served up immediately as some people fantasize that they would be.

Here I choose to consider that the creature reports should be examined as one more unusual bird appearing in West Virginia. The most detailed summary of the West Virginia events appeared in Keel's article in *Flying Saucer Review*. More reports were gathered together than could be explained by any one thing, but at the core of people-Mothman encounters there seems to be a bird of unusual size and behavior, a bird seen almost exclusively at night.

This bird, Bighoot, is unlike the Thunderbird in appearance and resembles an extremely large owl, larger than any known living owl. According to accounts in southwestern West Virginia and nearby parts of Ohio, the birds are brown and gray in color, with wingspans of about 10 feet (3 meters). The birds stand several feet tall. "Glowing red" eyes are reported. Red eye-shine is not exclusive to owls among the birds, but it is characteristic of owls. Seen from the rear they give the appearance of having no head. They reportedly make squeaking sounds.

The cover of darkness has been a big assist to giant owls in avoiding detection and identification. For daytime safety the birds appear to have developed effective camouflage. This method of concealment is already recognized among owls. Author Lewis Wayne Walker gave his personal observation of this method when observing long-eared owls. "One, perching on a broken branch, followed each movement through eyelids closed to mere slits. Clamping every feather to its body it assumed a sticklike appearance and feather tufts were raised to their utmost height creating an illusion startlingly like a broken log—even to the jagged splinters that might protrude from the top. The normal coloration of this owl matches the bark, so with erect stance to further heighten the protective mimicry, this pair had everything combined with a dramatic sense of timing which enhanced the effectiveness of each act." [18]

This mimicry in use by a giant owl was described by one witness to a creature reported in southern Ohio. The woman was at Rocky Fork Lake in August 1982. A year later she saw a similar sight at that lake. Her account made its way into *Bigfoot Co-Op* for October 1988.

> . . . . while fishing in Rocky Fork Lake in Ohio we drifted into a pristine cove on the SW side and noted with utter disbelief an old tall topless tree trunk approx 9-10 feet [2.7-3 meters] high, 112 inches [284 centimeters] around, move about 4 ft. [1.2 meters] sidewise. (This was on shore about 20 ft. [6 meters] inland among like-looking trees, with underbrush.) Again it moved only this time there was a partial twisting or rotation from the top 18-24 inches [45-60 centimeters]. It slowly maneuvered backward (keeping erect like a tree) into the woods with NO NOISES from it or underbrush as graceful as a bird thru a tree. It stopped in the mid of a sunlight clearing. . . .

She next wrote that "wings unfolded with a span greater than most small airplanes." It then returned to its "tree appearance." She could see the "semblance of two eyes" and it appeared to be watching them in their boat. They lost sight of it when the sun set. Then: "One year later, same lake, and a half mile or so from that first cove this figure appeared near shoreline again. (It seemed taller or leaner.) This time [I] got a look at its legs and feet—yellowish grainy like chicken legs. . . . They were so thin and short for its height. Three <u>long</u> slender toes with a hooked toe or nail on lower leg. (I won't swear to toes being 3 or 4.). . . ." [19]

The writer did not know what she saw and simply gave

these descriptions. It appears that she was seeing two different giant owls that were watching her as she was observing them.

People are still seeing giant owls because I hear about them, and the reports come from scattered locations. This isn't surprising because the birds are highly mobile creatures.

They appear likely to be a widespread species of bird as I have been hearing about them in many places over the years. They are simply a taboo topic in polite conversation, since they aren't supposed to exist. I have had people tell me of encounters with such enormous owls in Minnesota and Ohio. In those cases the owls were said to be white in color. The witnesses didn't think they were seeing snowy owls. What they saw was far too big.

People do not wish to go on record, and there's no place to go with their stories. Birdwatchers, naturally, want to see a bird for themselves, not hear about someone else's once-in-a-lifetime good fortune. Ornithologists want hard evidence such as feathers, photographs, and the like, not hearsay. If someone wants to complain that there is a lack of reports of such birds we can recognize that this is a narrow-minded response that doesn't acknowledge the prejudice that has been generated against unusual bird reports.

There are hints elsewhere in the world that giant owls might be found in places such as the UK and Chile. Again there has been no survey of the entire world for such giant birds, so these locations need not be singled out as the only places where the birds might be. They are simply the instances of sightings and folklore that have so far come to light.

Those birds in the United Kingdom were mentioned in chapter 13. In Chile, there have been reports of something called the Chon-chon. According to *Mythology of All Races*: "The Chon-chon, a vampire having the form of a human head whose huge ears serve as wings for its nocturnal flights, is reminiscent of the traveling heads which form so important a group of bogeys on the North American continent." [20]

The record of controversial topics like Bighoot indicates that it takes about a hundred years for something this elusive to become scientifically accepted. I have advocated the existence of Bighoot only since 1988. Given the slow pace for such things, it could easily take another 85 years for evidence to accumulate. [21] And beyond that point it might take more years for the survival of these birds to become generally accepted as fact. In an age of "fast-everything," people have little patience for such resolutions, but that is the nature of difficult questions in natural history. They take time to be resolved, and anyone with a serious interest in these issues should be aware of this condition.

Until then, these wonderful birds will continue to survive in their desired obscurity—for that is part of their survival strategy. They seem to have a well-developed camouflage that helps to keep them out of sight. Other characteristics argue for their continued presence in the wilds of North America and wherever they have survived around the world. Giant owl features are their confinement to nighttime activity, their great mobility as avian creatures, and their likely ability to vary their diet based upon whatever small animals are currently abundant in their surroundings.

I am less concerned for the survival of Bighoot than I am for the personal safety of anyone who would carelessly harass these formidable birds. They are "sleeping giants" in their environment. At present, they are no trouble to humans. But if provoked they're capable of using their skills with wings and claws to do harm to humans. So let us study these birds carefully at a distance when we venture to learn more about them. With prudence we surely can learn a lot more about these magnificent creatures without doing harm to them or to ourselves.

CHAPTER 16

The Challenges of Giant Birds of Prey

WE HAVE SEEN THAT THE PRESENCE OF GIANT BIRDS of prey is not a new phenomenon for North America and for the world at large. As we have looked further back in time the sightings of recent centuries meld into the record called folklore. Not so many years ago, people didn't know what these birds could be. In addition, no one cared about keeping a record of giant birds. The birds were viewed by American Indians as a menace to people and livestock and as competition for food sources in the wild. Competition in times of plenty would have been negligible. In times of scarcity, though, it would have been harmful to people and resented by them.

We cannot draw a lot of conclusions about the ways of these birds from the sparse record that we have now. In history and prehistory they were marginalized. They have so faded in importance that almost no one sees them as worthy of attention. Only a few cryptozoologists have been faithful to humankind's curiosity and have insisted that the stories of these wonders make sense and that the birds still exist. The winged beasts are simply rare. Even the bird-watchers—on whom some people seem to rely for their view that the birds are extinct—do not even know what constitutes a Thunderbird or a Bighoot so that they could know one if they saw it at almost any distance. Beyond that point, they are not allowed to speak up about what they see without conclusive evidence.

There seems to be universal agreement that conclusive evidence would be nice to have. There seems to be a lack of appreciation for how difficult conclusive evidence is to obtain in the real world. Living fossils like these birds are orphans in the realm of zoology. Anyone who thinks these topics have been screened by professional scientists and found wanting is dreaming. Ornithologists have dismissed these topics out of hand.

Consider how few people have actually seen whooping cranes, California condors, and Eskimo curlews. There is no doubt about their existence. They are birds that once were more numerous. They have declined to the point where few people get to see them in their living plumage. The giant birds of prey discussed here have gone beyond that kind of rarity. They appear to be on the edge of disappearing altogether.

Some people are happy with the notion that North America has been thoroughly put to a bulldozer blade, leaving no space for animals that are not represented in a zoo. If that is your conviction, I can do nothing for you. You will have to see one of these rarities for yourself. If that is your luck then your education will be complete. There will be very few people with whom you will be able to share the experience, for you will then be regarded as an unreliable person who sees things others cannot abide.

What is new in our times is a willingness to preserve and examine stories of strange animals. Among the benefits of the present age is that we have better record keeping all the time, including personal recollections and newspaper reporting. We also have better knowledge of prehistory through the accumulation of fossil discoveries.

It also is not an idea unique to giant birds that creatures known only from fossils might still survive in wild places that nature provides. Many other living fossils have been reported as still walking, swimming, and flying about the planet. This situation has given birth to the activity called "cryptozoology," where living things that are rare, doubted, or too strange to be considered credible are catalogued pending the appearance of conclusive proof. These rare animals are suspected to exist but are unconfirmed by zoologists. Such animals are hard to capture and therefore zoologists' need for a specimen has not yet been met. Numerous examples of this kind of animal (called a "cryptid") have been catalogued by George Eberhart in his encyclopedic two-volume work *Mysterious Creatures*. [1] Birds are one category of a vast field of open questions about elusive wildlife.

However, in the world of public opinion into which these subjects have been shooshed by nervous ornithologists, one man's evidence is another person's hogwash. Personally, I find the explanation of surviving fossil birds to be obvious and some of the easiest to accept in all of cryptozoology. Others have refused to acknowledge that some issues might be more difficult than proving the existence of robins or penguins. They want a dead body whenever it is needed, and they haven't seen one, so forget it. Whether we really need a dead body in these cases will be taken up again a little further on.

If we take history as our guide we can suggest that these topics will, after some decades, be made whole and plain to one and all. The recent history of such issues of this kind shows that they progress from early advocacy through a period of growing attention. Eventually, after many decades, they become more respectable.

There might have been an early interest in Thunderbirds by an ornithologist late in the 19th century, but that person appears not to have gone on record with his views.

The modern record of Thunderbirds—as opposed to the storytelling versions of Indian accounts and the mistaken perceptions of super-eagles—began with the sighting of a Thunderbird by Robert Lyman Sr. around 1940. From that point on, the big birds became part of Pennsylvania history. Bob Lyman knew they existed, and he interviewed others with personal experiences with the birds. Lyman wrote up these accounts in his book *Amazing Indeed*. The rest of us have followed in his footsteps in trying to learn more about these spectacular creatures.

From that small base, the number of people who are aware of the persistence of the birds has grown, thanks to the publicity for the sightings of giant birds. In books and articles, the birds have been promoted and then portrayed as a surviving fossil bird. A few more decades will probably pass before the living Thunderbirds are recognized as part of nature in the Americas.

The behavior of the Thunderbirds is such that they will make themselves apparent by some kind of attack upon a human or humans in the normal course of their pursuit of prey. The record shows that this happens every few decades in a way that generates publicity. Such an incident or incidents are potential learning opportunities. But history also has shown us that these opportunities pass without our understanding them. No one has the means or the obligation to make sense of the opportunities to track the birds, observe the birds, and attempt to verify their nature and very existence. In the last part of the 20th century, the birds were scarcely remembered. An interest in such birds among amateur bird-watchers could be helpful, but this interest hasn't been demonstrated so far.

Giant owls have suffered the same neglect as the Thunderbirds. They made an early appearance in history as "Booger Owls" or as even more obscure and misunderstood entities. The distortion of calling them "Flying Heads" among the Iroquois was only matched when, in the 20th century, they were thought to have come from outer space.

Because the presence of Bighoot has only been advocated for a quarter of a century, we have little expectation that the owls will soon be recognized and studied. It will take much longer for their presence to be accepted. If some effort were made to study them, for nothing has been done to date, we could begin to understand something of the way they live and how they have survived. If they don't become extinct, we might know them better by the end of the 21st century. Life is tenacious—so much so that I would bet that these birds will be around that long.

How can we make any progress in learning about these birds? The first thing we need to do is to start talking about them. Let more people know that such things could be around and would be legitimate to report. If people were permitted the opportunity to put these kinds of birds on record, then we could begin the search for them in earnest.

Their appearance, their habits, their range of activities, and their choices of prey could all be outlined from the collection of detailed reports about encounters with them.

Nesting sites must exist, however remote they might be for Thunderbirds or however insubstantial the owls' might be. A lot could be learned from the study of abandoned nesting sites. Feathers, eggshells, and remains of prey could be obtained and analyzed.

I have been urging that the best approach to all these amazing survivals in the animal kingdom would be to study them at a distance. The zoologists' desire for a specimen is understandable. But in the cases of uncataloged cryptids, beginning with a specimen isn't practical.

These animals are rare and canny and well aware of the danger we pose to their freedom of activity. Some have been killed in the past, but not many. This would be the case because they are few in numbers and hardy survivors when tangling with other animals.

We have reached a stage in identifying animal life where the easy questions have been dispatched. Now we need to use our smarts to cope with the difficult questions where animal specimens are not easily obtained with a gun or a trap.

We can start with a historical summary such as the one I have presented here. We can add more information by allowing, soliciting, and recording people's genuine experiences with giant birds of prey.

I had a discussion with a professional scientist some years ago, who said, "You have to play by the rules." My response was, "No you don't. You change the rules." The existence of creatures like Thunderbirds and giant owls require us to come up with new rules. The old ways of "Shoot 'em and bag 'em" reach their limit when the animals are canny and capable of avoiding our usual expectations.

New rules are needed because we have failed to identify and learn about two of the largest birds in the world by using the old rules. It makes no sense—it is decidedly foolish, in fact—to insist that we should stick to old rules and therefore continue the confusion about what is going on around us.

There are many creatures still around that don't permit us the luxury of just banging away to take home a specimen. They can be rare. They can be elusive. They can be too big to catch. They can be too smart or too well adapted to their environment. They can be too like us to raise ethical issues of near-homicidal conduct if we were to use the old methods. If we use our brains instead of gun-powder, we might make some progress in learning about giant sea creatures, giant land animals in mountains, giant things in swamps, and giant birds in remote mountains and forests.

One of the best arguments for the existence of Thunderbirds is the Lowe incident of 1977. No one has come up with an expla-nation for that occurrence and its logical context of sightings, other than the annual passage of migrating Thunderbirds. The lame excuse of turkey vultures is simply a splendid example of how hard it is for some people to learn. They will accept any proposition that doesn't involve something new and doesn't require them to expand their understanding of the world of nature.

As we have seen, the presence of Thunderbirds is not new. They have been around for a long time in every conceivable con-text—as fossils, in folklore, and in the history of North America.

One of the challenges we face is to overcome the voices of despair that insult anyone who has seen something that they haven't seen for themselves. Some birds are common. Many of them can be seen by going to the right place at the right time. Other birds can be rare and be seen by only a few lucky people who come upon them unprepared for the experience.

Such has been the case for the observers of the Thunderbirds and the sighters of Bighoot. They are a fortunate group who has had an experience few will easily share.

Professional scientists have refused to take an active interest in these birds. In doing so, they simply perpetuate their own myth that there are no new animals to be found in North America. The birds are there for those with the sense and the curiosity to look for them. Two of the largest birds in the world await formal discovery as living creatures. May they prosper and continue to share this planet with us for all time.

ACKNOWLEDGMENTS

I HAVE HAD THE ASSISTANCE OF MANY PEOPLE IN gathering together the records of mysterious birds.

The staffs of many small town and larger community newspapers in the US have responded to appeals for help and helped to create this book.

I particularly want to express my gratitude to those people who have given their time and assistance because of their own curiosity about the world around us and their willingness to let the facts take us wherever they must.

My special thanks to Loren Coleman, Jerry Coleman, Benoit Crevier, Judith Diliberto, Rod B. Dyke, Lou Farish, Joan Jeffers, Paul G. Johnson, Wanda and Joseph Kaye, Robert Lyman Sr., Carl Masthay, Clyde Mincer, Gerald Musinsky, John Rasmussen, and Alan R. Woolworth.

NOTES

Chapter 1. They Came from the Sky

1. Anchorage DAILY TIMES, 18 October 2002.
2. Allison Jornlin, "The Brookfield Thunderbird (1988)," at www.weird-wi.com. Posted 3 July 2001.
3. John Jennings, "Bigfoot Returns," BLAIRSVILLE DISPATCH at www.pittsburghlive.com. 31 January 2003.
4. To reconstruct the events of 25 July through 11 August 1977 the author canvassed 35 newspaper publishers in Illinois from Peoria to Mt. Vernon during those months. Information was received from 15 of them. Newspapers from Chicago and other major cities were consulted. The author also received assistance from the Shelbyville office of the U.S. Army Corps of Engineers.
5. Bloomington PANTAGRAPH, 27 July 1977.
6. Chicago DAILY NEWS, 27 July 1977, Red Streak Edition.
7. United Press International, 28 July 1977, Miami (Florida) HERALD.
8. Lincoln COURIER, 28 July 1977.
9. Springfield STATE JOURNAL-REGISTER, 27 July 1977.
10. Lincoln COURIER, 26 July 1977.
11. Pekin DAILY TIMES, 30 July 1977.
12. Bloomington PANTAGRAPH, 27 July 1977.
13. Springfield STATE JOURNAL-REGISTER, 27 July 1977.
14. Lincoln COURIER, 28 July 1977.
15. Ibid.

Chapter 2. They Are Seen Again

1. Pekin DAILY TIMES, 20 July 1977.
2. Bloomington PANTAGRAPH, 2 August 1977.
3. Bloomington PANTAGRAPH, 29 July 1977.
4. United Press International, 30 July 1977, and Bloomington PANTAGRAPH, 29 July 1977.
5. Pekin DAILY TIMES, 30 July 1977.
6. Bloomington PANTGRAPH, 29 July 1977.
7. Lincoln COURIER, 4 August 1977.

8. Bloomington PANTAGRAPH, 29 July 1977 and 30 July 1977, and Peoria JOURNAL STAR, 30 July 1977.

9. Bloomington PANTAGRAPH, 31 July 1977.

10. United Press International, 1 August 1977, and Champaign-Urbana COURIER, 1 August 1977.

11. Bloomington PANTAGRAPH, 31 July 1977.

12. Bloomington PANTAGRAPH, 1 August 1977.

13. Bloomington PANTAGRAPH, 2 August 1977.

14. E.C. Brewer, THE DICTIONARY OF PHRASE AND FABLE, reprinted. (NY: Avenel Books, 1978), 891-2.

15. Chicago SUN-TIMES, 12 August 1977.

16. Centralia SENTINEL, 11 August 1977.

17. Ibid.

Chapter 3. Another Nine-Day Wonder

1. UPI dispatch, Pekin DAILY TIMES, 28 July 1977.

2. Decatur HERALD, 28 July 1977.

3. AP dispatch, Kansas City TIMES, 1 August 1977, and AP dispatch, Milwaukee SENTINEL, 1 August 1977.

4. Chicago TRIBUNE, 4 August 1977.

5. AP dispatch, St. Louis GLOBE-DEMOCRAT, 3 August 1977, and AP dispatch, Des Moines REGISTER, 3 August 1977.

6. Mount Pulaski TIMES-NEWS, 4 August 1977.

7. Des Moines REGISTER, 9 August 1977.

8. Peoria JOURNAL-STAR, 31 July 1977.

9. Chicago TRIBUNE, 2 August 1977, Milwaukee SENTINEL, 1 August 1977 and 2 August 1977, and Milwaukee JOURNAL, 2 August 1977.

10. Milwaukee SENTINEL, 2 August 1977.

11. Springfield STATE JOURNAL-REGISTER, 27 July 1977.

12. Bloomington PANTAGRAPH, 27 July 1977.

13. Chicago DAILY NEWS, 27 July 1977 and 30-31 July 1977.

14. Chicago TRIBUNE, 30 July 1977.

15. Peoria JOURNAL-STAR, 30 July 1977.

16. Pekin DAILY TIMES, 30 July 1977.

17. AP dispatch, Des Moines REGISTER, 3 August 1977.

18. "DOC seeks Word on 'Big Bird'" in OUTDOOR HIGHLIGHTS 5(24): (8 August 1977).

19. St. Louis POST-DISPATCH, 9 April 1948.

20. St. Louis POST-DISPATCH for the dates of 10-13 April, 25-26 April, 28-30 April, 1-3 May, 6 May 1948. For details of these reports see Loren E. Coleman, CURIOUS ENCOUNTERS (Boston: Faber and Faber, 1985), 32-37.

21. Charles Fort, THE BOOKS OF CHARLES FORT (NY: Holt, 1941).

22. Loren E. Coleman, MYSTERIOUS AMERICA—THE REVISED EDITION (NY: Paraview Press, 2001), 22-4.

23. Perry A. Armstrong, Springfield STATE JOURNAL-REGISTER, 27 July 1977.

Chapter 4. Birds that Carry Off People

1. Jacques Pearl ("Jack Pearl"), "Monster Bird that Carries off Human Beings," SAGA, May 1963, 29-31, 83-85.

2. Felix A. Pouchet, THE UNIVERSE (New York: Scribner, 1871), 255.

3. David Jacobsen, THE AFFAIRS OF DAME RUMOR (NY: Rinehart & Co., 1948), 27-31.

4. "Fake Eagle Stories," NATURE MAGAZINE (Washington, DC), 27:106 (1936); Lee W. Arnold, "Eagle Attacks Boy," AUDUBON MAGAZINE, 50(4):356-7 (July August 1948).

Chapter 5. The Mystery of the Balds

1. Perry A. Armstrong, THE PIASA, OR, THE DEVIL AMONG THE INDIANS (Morris, IL: 1887); John W. Allen, LEGENDS AND LORE OF SOUTHERN ILLINOIS (Carbondale, IL: Southern Illinois University, 1963), 104-6; John Bakeless, THE EYES OF DISCOVERY (New York: Dover, 1961), 331-34; Tom English, "The Piasa Petroglyph: The Devourer from the Bluffs," ART AND ARCHAEOLOGY 14(3):151-56 (September 1922); Federal Writers' Project, THE WPA GUIDE TO ILLINOIS (New York: Pantheon Books, 1983), 153-54; AP dispatch, Niagara Falls (NY) GAZETTE, 1 April 1927; Harry Hansen, ed. ILLINOIS: A DESCRIPTIVE AND HISTORICAL GUIDE (New York: Hastings House, 1974), 137-8;

Henry Lewis, THE VALLEY OF THE MISSSISSIPPI ILLUSTRATED, edited with an introduction and notes by Bertha L. Heilbron (St. Paul: Minnesota Historical Society, 1967).

2. Bakeless, EYES OF DISCOVERY, 331.
3. FWP, WPA GUIDE TO ILLINOIS, 154.
4. Lewis, VALLEY OF THE MISSISSIPPI ILLUSTRATED, 281n.14.
5. English, "The Piasa Petroglyph," 152, 154.
6. Niagara Falls (NY) GAZETTE, 1 April 1927.
7. Francis Parkman, THE DISCOVERY OF THE GREAT WEST 10th ed. (Boston : Little, Brown, and Company, 1878), 59. Parkman made these observations on the "The Painted Rocks" at Alton:

The rock where these figures were painted is immediately above the city of Alton. The tradition of their existence remains, though they are entirely effaced by time. In 1867, when I passed the place, a part of the rock had been quarried away, and, instead of Marquette's monsters, it bore a huge advertisement of "Plantation Bitters." Some years ago, certain persons, with more zeal than knowledge, proposed to restore the figures, after conceptions of their own; but the idea was abandoned.

Marquette made a drawing of the monsters, but it is lost. I have, however, a facsimile of a map made a few years later by order of the Intendant Duchesneau; which is decorated with the portrait of one of them, answering to Marquette's description, and probably copied from his drawing. St. Cosme, who saw them in 1699, says that they were even then almost effaced. Douay and Joutel also speak of them; the former, bitterly hostile to his Jesuit contemporaries, charging Marquette with exaggeration in his account of them. Joutel could see nothing terrifying in their appearance; but he says that his Indians made sacrifices to them as they passed.

8. English, "The Piasa Petroglyph," 152-53.
9. Paul G. Brewster, "The Piasa Bird: A Legend of the Illini," HOOSIER FOLKLORE 7:83-6 (1949).

THUNDERBIRDS

10. English, "The Piasa Petroglyph," 154-5.

11. Ibid., 155.

12. Federal Writers' Project, SOUTH CAROLINA; A GUIDE TO THE PAL-METTO STATE (New York: Oxford University Press, 1941), 346.

13. Vance Randolph, WE ALWAYS LIE TO STRANGERS (New York: Columbia University Press, 1951), 63-66.

14. Atlanta (Georgia) CONSTITUTION, 5 November 1975.

15. Ross E. Hutchins, HIDDEN VALLEY OF THE SMOKIES: WITH A NAT-URALIST IN THE GREAT SMOKY MOUNTAINS (New York: Dodd, Mead, 1971), 208-9.

16. Edwin Way Teale, NORTH WITH THE SPRING (New York: Dodd, Mead, 1951), 190-6.

17. Bill Sharpe, TAR ON MY HEELS: A PRESS AGENT'S NOTE BOOK (Winston-Salem: The Tar Heels, 1946), 123-24.

18. Teale, NORTH WITH THE SPRING, 194.

19. Sharpe, TAR ON MY HEELS, 123-27.

20. Herbert Ravenel Sass, HEAR ME, MY CHIEFS! (New York: Morrow, 1940), 97-101.

21. James Mooney, "Myths of the Cherokee," ANNUAL REPORT, BUREAU OF AMERICAN ETHNOLOGY No. 19, 1897-1898, 315-6, 466.

Chapter 6. Sky Kings of the Past

1. Stansbury Hagar, "Micmac Customs and Traditions," AMERICAN ANTHROPOLOGIST, o.s., 8:41-42 (January 1895).

2. Mooney, "Myths of the Cherokee," 316.

3. J. Clarence Webster, AN HISTORICAL GUIDE TO NEW BRUNSWICK, rev. ed. (New Brunswick Government Bureau of Information and Tourist Travel, 1947).

4. Edward Jack, "Maliseet Legends," JOURNAL OF AMERICAN FOLKLORE 8:200-1 (1895).

5. Charles Leland, THE ALGONKIN LEGENDS OF NEW ENGLAND (Boston: Houghton Mifflin, 1884).

6. Frank G. Speck, "Montagnais and Naskapi Tales from the Labrador Peninsula," JOURNAL OF AMERICAN FOLKLORE 38:9 (1925).

7. Apheus Hyatt Verrill, ALONG NEW ENGLAND SHORES (NY: Putnam, 1936), 138.

8. Washington Matthews, "Navaho Legends," MEMOIRS OF THE AMERICAN FOLKLORE SOCIETY 5:119-20 (1897).

9. Richard Barber and Anne Riches, A DICTIONARY OF FABULOUS BEASTS (New York: Walker, 1971), 9.

10. NEW MEXICO MAGAZINE, 25(1):32 (January 1947). More about Capulin Mountain can be found in NEW MEXICO SUN TRAILS 7(5):17-18 (June 1954).

11. Hartley B. Alexander, MYTHOLOGY OF ALL RACES: NORTH AMERICAN (1916; reprint, New York: Cooper Square, 1964), X:139.

12. Elmer Sparks, "A New Mystery on the Donner Trail," FRONTIER TIMES (Winter 1960), 27, 41-2.

13. Campbell Grant, ROCK ART OF THE AMERICAN INDIAN (New York: Crowell, 1967), 58-59, 124, 131, 149; and Garrick Mallery, "Pictographs of the North American Indians—A Preliminary Paper," BUREAU OF AMERICAN ETHNOLOGY, ANNUAL REPORT 4:188-90 (1882-83).

14. A.F. Chamberlain, "The Thunderbird Amongst the Algonkins," AMERICAN ANTHROPOLOGIST, o.s., 3:51 (January 1890).

15. Ibid.

16. Kelsie B. Harder, ILLUSTRATED DICTIONARY OF PLACE NAMES: UNITED STATES AND CANADA (New York: Van Nostrand Reinhold, 1976), 547.

17. Chamberlain, "Thunderbird Amongst the Algonkins," 51.

18. George Laidlaw, "Ojibway Myths and Tales," ONTARIO ARCHAEOLOGICAL REPORT 1915, Ontario Provincial Museum, Toronto, 72.

19. Theresa S. Smith, THE ISLAND OF THE ANISHNAABEG (Moscow, ID: University of Idaho Press, 1995), 80-81.

20. Dorothy Moulding Brown, WISCONSIN INDIAN PLACE-NAME LEGENDS, 1948 series, pp. 20-21.

21. Ibid., 26-27.

22. Alanson Skinner and John V. Satterlee, "Folklore of the Menomini Indians," ANTHROPOLOGICAL PAPERS AMERICAN MUSEUM OF NATURAL HISTORY 13:488-90 (1915).

23. Theodore H. Lewis, "Ancient Rock Inscriptions in Eastern Dakota," AMERICAN NATURALIST 20:423-24 (1886). "Devil's Nest" appears on p. 50 of MINNESOTA ATLAS & GAZETTEER (Freeport, ME: DeLorme Mapping, 1990). Daniel E. Willard describes the site in THE STORY OF THE PRAIRIES OR THE LANDSCAPE GEOLOGY OF NORTH DAKOTA 11th ed. (1926):

Rising conspicuously from the prairie south of Hankinson stands a large dune 150 feet high, covered scatteringly with trees, known as Lightning's Nest. A track of dunes from ten to thirty feet high and mostly covered with grass extends to the northwest. Lightning's Nest has been built up from the sands of the Herman Shore-Line, where it crosses the Sheyenne Delta. The Norcross Beach passes close east of Hankinson as a well defined sand ridge. The hills of the Dovre Moraine are a prominent range south and west (p.360).

24. George Laidlaw, "Ojibway Myths and Tales," ONTARIO ARCHAEOLOGICAL REPORT 1915, 1916, 1918, Ontario Provincial Museum, Toronto; Harlan I. Smith, "Some Ojibwa Myths and Traditions," JOURNAL OF AMERICAN FOLKLORE 19:219-20 (1906); and Mary Eastman, DACOTAH: LIFE AND LEGENDS OF THE SIOUX (1849; reprint, Minneapolis: Ross & Haines, 1962).

25. Stanley Vestal, SHORT GRASS COUNTRY (New York: Duell, Sloan, & Pearce, 1941), 142.

26. James Mooney, "The Ghost Dance Religion," BUREAU OF AMERICAN ETHNOLOGY, ANNUAL REPORT 14, pt. 2:968-69 (1892-93).

27. Claude E. Schaeffer, "Was the California Condor Known to the Blackfoot Indians?" JOURNAL OF THE WASHINGTON ACADEMY OF SCIENCES 41:181-91 (June 1951).

28. John C. Ewers, THE STORY OF THE BLACKFEET (Washington, D.C.: U.S. Department of the Interior, 1944), 7-8.

29. Franz Boas, "Kutenai Tales," BUREAU OF AMERICAN ETHNOLOGY, BULLETIN 59 (1918): 286.

30. Author interview with Rene Dahinden, February 1980.

31. Dale Ott, "Thunder in their Wings," NORTHWEST MAGAZINE (supplement to the OREGONIAN, Portland), 28 March 1971, 6-7.

32. C. Hart Merriam, THE DAWN OF THE WORLD (Cleveland: Arthur Clark, 1910; reprinted 1993 by University of Nebraska Press, Lincoln), 163.

33. William H. Dall, "On Masks, Labrets, and Certain Aboriginal Customs, with an Inquiry into the Bearing of their Geographical Distribution," BUREAU OF AMERICAN ETHNOLOGY, ANNUAL REPORT 3 (1881-82): 329-36.

34. Eells, "The Thunderbird,"330.

35. Albert Reagan and L. V. W. Walters, "Tales of the Hoh and Quileute," JOURNAL OF AMERICAN FOLKLORE 46:320-2 (1933).

36. Deborah Easter, "Thunderbird: Storm God of the Northwest," PACIFIC SEARCH 12:19 (July-August 1978).

37. Ronald L. Olson, THE QUINAULT INDIANS (1936; reprint, Seattle: University of Washington Press, 1967), 169.

38. Eells, "The Thunderbird," 331.

39. Easter, "Thunderbird," 18.

40. Reader's Digest Association (Canada), CANADIAN BOOK OF THE ROAD (1980), No. 26.

41. James G. Swan, "The Haidah Indians of Queen Charlotte Islands, British Columbia," SMITHSONIAN CONTRIBUTIONS OF KNOWLEDGE NO. 267, 21:5 (1874), Plate 4.

42. John R. Swanton, "Social Condition, Beliefs, and Linguistic Relationship of the Tlingit Indians," BUREAU OF AMERICAN ETHNOLOGY, ANNUAL REPORT 26 (1904-05) 454.

43. Dall, "On Masks, Labrets," 119-20; and William H. Dall, ALASKA AND ITS RESOURCES (Boston: Lee and Shepard, 1870), 424.

44. Frederica de Laguna, "Under Mount Saint Elias," SMITHSONIAN CONTRIBUTIONS TO ANTHROPOLOGY 7:804 (1972).

45. Henry Rink, TALES AND TRADITIONS OF THE ESKIMO (Edinburgh: Blackwood, 1875), 259.

46. Dall, "On Masks, Labrets," 120.

47. Donald J. Orth, DICTIONARY OF ALASKA PLACE NAMES (Washington: GPO, 1967), 1004.

48. Edward W. Nelson, "The Eskimo About Bering Strait," BUREAU OF AMERICAN ETHNOLOGY, ANNUAL REPORT 8:486-87 (1896-97).

Chapter 7. Thunderbirds West

1. ALASKA Magazine, August 1972, p. 27.
2. Dan McCowan, ANIMALS OF THE CANADIAN ROCKIES (New York: Dodd, Mead, 1936), 270.
3. FATE, December 1954, pp. 128-9.
4. THE TRACK RECORD (Portland, OR), No. 58, June 1996, p. 8.
5. Richard Smith, CONDOR JOURNAL: THE HISTORY, MYTHOLOGY, AND REALITY OF THE CALIFORNIA CONDOR (Santa Barbara, California: Capra Press, 1978). 85-86.
6. Ott, "Thunder in Their Wings," 7.
7. Horace Bell, ON THE OLD WEST COAST (NY: Morrow, 1930), 202.
8. "Current Events: Thunderbirds," WONDERS 1(2):25 (June 1992).
9. Oakland (California) TRIBUNE, 16 January 1976.
10. St. Catherines (Ontario) EVENING JOURNAL, 20 September 1871.
11. DESERET NEWS (Salt Lake City, Utah), 18 July 1966.
12. United Press International, VALLEY MORNING STAR (Harlingen, Texas), 15 January 1976.
13. Ibid.
14. Palestine (Texas) HERALD-PRESS, 16, 19, 22 December 1976.
15. DOUBT No. 12, p. 175. DOUBT was the organ of the Fortean Society from 1932 to 1959.
16. Gladwell Richardson ("Maurice Kildare"), "Winged Terror in the Oklahoma Hills," TRUE FRONTIER, October 1972 (No. 29), pp. 29-30, 50, 52-53.

Chapter 8. Thunderbirds East

1. David St. Albans, "Update on Thunderbirds," World Explorer 1(5):8-11 (1994).
2. John D. Rasmussen, "This 'N' That" column in THE EXPRESS (Lock Haven, Pennsylvania), 8 June 1977, p. 13.
3. Atlanta CONSTITUTION, 18 September 1868.

4. Grant Callison, "Winged Creatures Over Illinois," CRUX (Paris, TX) No 2 (1986) pp. 12-13.

5. FATE, May 1961, pp. 16-17.

6. St. Paul (Minnesota) PRESS, 11 January 1870.

7. Cincinnati (Ohio) ENQUIRER, 18 and 19 May 1977, KENTUCKY POST (Cincinnati, Ohio), 18 May 1977; Cincinnati (Ohio) POST, 19 May 1977; and Associated Press, Lima (Ohio) NEWS, 18 May 1977.

8. FATE, August 1984, p. 37.

9. Lancaster (Ohio) EAGLE-GAZETTE, 8 and 23 August 1972.

10. RES BUREAU BULLETIN (Kingston, Ontario), 4 November 1976 (No.8), pp. 1-2.

11. Charleston (West Virginia) DAILY MAIL, 21 August 1978, pp. 1A, 4A.

12. Alyce T. Weinberg, "Ghost Stories of Frederick County, Maryland," 1973. p. 6, manuscript in the public library of Frederick, Maryland.

13. Page 105 in Jerome Clark, "Unidentified Flapping Objects," OUI Magazine, October 1976, pp. 94-98, 100, 105-6.

14. ESSEX COUNTY REPUBLICAN (Elizabethtown, New York), 27 September 1894.

15. Letter to the author from Judith Diliberto, 10 May 1989.

16. Jean Ferguson, LES HUMANNOIDES, LES CERVEAUX QUI DIRIGENT LES SOUCOUPES VOLANTES (Montreal: Editions Lemeac, 1977), 201-4.

17. Albert Russell Hart, "American Historical Liars," HARPER'S MONTHLY MAGAZINE 131:730-1 (October 1915).

Chapter 9. Pennsylvania Thunderbirds

1. Alice Ford, ed., AUDUBON, BY HIMSELF (Garden City, NY: Natural History Press, 1989), 154-5.

2. Victor E. Shelford, ed., NATURALIST'S GUIDE TO THE AMERICAS (Baltimore: Williams & Wilkins, 1926), 340.

3. Freeman Tilden, THE STATE PARKS: THEIR MEANING IN AMERICAN LIFE (NY: Knopf, 1962), 65-69.

4. Robert R. Lyman Sr., AMAZING INDEED: STRANGE EVENTS IN THE BLACK FOREST, VOLUME 2 (Coudersport, PA: The Potter Enterprise, 1973), 93-97.

5. Lyman's other books were FORBIDDEN LAND: STRANGE EVENTS IN THE BLACK FOREST, VOLUME 1; HISTORY OF ROULET, PA.; and THE LIFE AND TIMES OF MAJOR ISAAC LYMAN.

6. Letter to the author from Wanda Kaye, 2 January 1989.

7. Letter to the author from Clyde Mincer. 19 September 1977.

8. Letter to the editor of FATE from Hiram M. Cranmer, March 1966.

9. Letter to the editor of FATE from Hiram M. Cranmer, November 1956.

10. Gerald Musinsky, "The Return of the Thunderbirds," FATE, November 1995, pp. 48-51.

11. Letters to the editor of FATE from Hiram M. Cranmer, April 1958 and September 1963.

12 Letter to the editor of FATE from Hiram M. Cranmer, September 1963.

13. Letter to the author from Clyde Mincer letter, 19 September 1977. These observations were also described in Lyman, AMAZING INDEED, 96.

14. Letter to the author from Wanda Kaye, 2 January 1989.

15. Letter to the author from Robert Lyman Sr., 10 February 1974.

16. Curt Sutherly, "Great Birds of the Allegheny Plateau," CAVEAT EMPTOR, Winter 1989-90, p. 22.

17. Paul G. Johnson, CREATURE RESEARCH JOURNAL No. 9 (North Versailles, PA), Spring 1991, p.5.

Chapter 10. A Bird of Prey

1. Laidlaw, "Ojibway Myths and Tales," 1916, 90.

2. Lyman, AMAZING INDEED, 95.

3. James Deans, "The Thunder-Bird," AMERICAN ANTIQUARIAN AND ORIENTAL JOURNAL 7:357-8 (1885).

4. A. Landsborough Thomson, ed., A NEW DICTIONARY OF BIRDS (New York: McGraw-Hill, 1964), 353-4.

5. Glenys Lloyd and Derek Lloyd, BIRDS OF PREY (New York: Bantam, 1970), 44-47.

6. Mooney, "Myths of the Cherokee," 315, 316.

7. Brown, WISCONSIN PLACE-NAME LEGENDS, 21.

8. Nelson, "Eskimo About Bering Strait," 486.

9. Peoria (Illinois) JOURNAL STAR, 30 July 1977.

10. Mattoon (Illinois) JOURNAL GAZETTE, 1 August 1977.

11. United Press International, VALLEY MORNING STAR (Harlingen, Texas), 15 January 1976.

12. Lyman, AMAZING INDEED, 96.

13. George E. Lankford, ed. NATIVE AMERICAN LEGENDS (Little Rock: August House, 1987), 75.

14. James Owen Dorsey, "A Study of Siouan Cults," BUREAU OF AMERICAN ETHNOLOGY, ANNUAL REPORT 11 (1889-90):442 (Washington: GPO, 1894; Albert S. Gatschet, "Water Monsters of the American Aborigines," JOURNAL OF AMERICAN FOLKLORE 12:255-60 (1899); and Colin F. Taylor, ed., NATIVE AMERICAN MYTHS AND LEGENDS (London: Salamander Books, 1994), 18, 47, 89.

15. Mark A. Hall, "Lake Michigan Monsters," WONDERS 2(2):36-45 (June 1993).

16. Edwin Bernbaum, SACRED MOUNTAINS OF THE WORLD (San Francisco: Sierra Club Books, 1990), 156. The original source is William K. Powers, SACRED LANGUAGE: THE NATURE OF SUPERNATURAL DISCOURSE IN LAKOTA (Norman: University of Oklahoma Press, 1986), 37.

17. Federal Writers' Project, NEBRASKA: A GUIDE TO THE CORNHUSKER STATE (NY: Hastings House, 1939), 396.

18. Chamberlain, "Thunderbird Amongst the Algonkins," 52.

19. Smith, ISLAND OF THE ANISHNAABEG, 80-81.

20. Dorothy Moulding Brown, "Legends of the Wisconsin Hills," WISCONSIN ARCHEOLOGIST 18(l):17-21 (December 1937).

21. Robert E. Gard and L.G. Sorden, WISCONSIN LORE (Stanton and Lee Publishers, 1962), 45, 186-88.

22. Brown, "Wisconsin Hills," 17.

23. W. J. Hoffman, "Mythology of the Menomini Indians," AMERICAN ANTHROPOLOGIST 3:244 (July 1890).

24. Gard and Sorden, WISCONSIN LORE, 51-55.

25. ILLINOIS ATLAS & GAZETTEER (Freeport, ME: DeLorme, 1991).

26. Randolph, WE ALWAYS LIE, 63-64.

27. Otto Ernest Rayburn, OZARK COUNTRY (NY: Duell, Sloan & Pearce, 1941), 308-10.

28. Randolph, WE ALWAYS LIE, 64-65.

Chapter 11. A Fortean Problem

1. Angelo P. Caparella, CRYPTOZOOLOGY 9:94-96 (1990) and 10:116-7 (1991).
2. Vestal, SHORT GRASS COUNTRY, 142.
3. Mooney, "Ghost Dance Religion," 968-9.
4. Eastman, DAHCOTAH, 191.
5. Richardson, "Winged Terror," 53.
6. Schaeffer, "Was the Condor Known," 184, 185.
7. Ibid., 184.
8. Ibid., 187.
9. St. Paul (Minnesota) PRESS, 11 January 1870.
10. Lyman, AMAZING INDEED, 95.
11. Olson, THE QUINAULT INDIANS, 169.
12. F.W. Hodge, ed., "Handbook of the American Indians North of Mexico," BUREAU OF AMERICAN ETHNOLOGY, BULLETIN 30 (1907-1910): 746-7.
13. Easter, "Thunderbird," 19.
14. Sparks, "New Mystery on the Donner Trail," 41-42.

Chapter 12. Photographic Evidence

1. Champaign-Urbana (Illinois) COURIER, 1 August 1977.
2. Ibid.; and Lincoln (Illinois) COURIER, 1 August 1977.
3. Tuscola (Illinois) JOURNAL, 2 August 1977.
4. Chicago (Illinois) SUN-TIMES, 3 August 1977.
5. Tombstone (Arizona Territory) EPITAPH, 26 April 1890, p. 3 col. 6.
6. Bell, ON THE OLD WEST COAST, 204-5.
7. J. K. Parrish, "Our Country's Mysterious Monsters," OLD WEST 6(l):25, 37 (Fall 1969).
8. Letter to the editor from Harry F. McClure, OLD WEST 6(4):2 (Summer 1970).
9. "Prehistoric Survivors," MAN AND BEAST (Pleasantville, NY: Reader's Digest, 1993), 31-33.

10. Pearl, "Monster Bird," 84.

11. Letters to the editor from Hiram M. Cranmer, FATE, December 1950, pp. 91, 93,95; November 1956, pp. 122-4; April 1958, pp. 128-9; September 1963, pp. 116-7; March 1966, pp. 131-2.

12. "Thunderbirds again—and again," PURSUIT, April 1972, pp. 40-41, and "Society News," PURSUIT, January 1969, p. 17.

13. Letter to the editor from Wayne Winters, FATE, August 1966, pp. 128-9.

14. "Big Bird a Tall Tale," Tombstone (Arizona) EPITAPH (National Edition), November 1984.

15. Letter to the editor from W. Ritchie Benedict, FATE, October 1974, pp. 131-2.

16. John Keel, "Beyond the Known," FATE, March 1991, p. 19.

Chapter 13. Ancient Terrors from the Skies

1. C. Leonard-Stuart and George Hagar, eds., EVERYBODY'S CYCLOPE-DIA (New York: Syndicate Publishing Co, 1912), V, under "Thunderbird."

2. Ernest Ingersoll, BIRDS IN LEGEND, FABLE AND FOLKLORE (NY: Longmans, Green, 1923), 247.

3. Edward A. Armstrong, THE LIFE AND LORE OF THE BIRD (NY: Crown, 1975), 76-78.

4. Ibid., 89.

5. Marco Polo, THE TRAVELS OF MARCO POLO THE VENETIAN (London: J. M. Dent & Co., 1908); Henry Yule, tr. and ed., BOOK OF SER MARCO POLO, 2nd ed. (London: 1875), II, 404-14; and Richard Carrington, "Fabulous Birds" in A. Landsborough Thomson, ed., A NEW DICTIONARY OF THE BIRDS (NY: McGraw-Hill, 1964), 265-6.

6. Ingersoll, BIRDS IN LEGEND, 202.

7. Ibid., 191-211; and Joe Nigg, A GUIDE TO THE IMAGINARY BIRDS OF THE WORLD (Cambridge, MA: Apple-Wood Books, 1984).

8. James Clarke, MAN IS THE PREY (NY: Stein & Day, 1969), 247.

9. Alfred Newton, A DICTIONARY OF BIRDS (London: 1896), 791-3.

10. Polo, TRAVELS OF MARCO POLO, 394.

11. Yule, BOOK OF SER MARCO POLO, II, 413-4.

12. Ibid., II, 409.

13. Newton, DICTIONARY OF BIRDS, 286n.

14. Bernard Heuvelmans, ON THE TRACK OF UNKNOWN ANIMALS (NY: Hill and Wang, 1958), 485-95; Ivan T. Sanderson, INVESTIGATING THE UNEXPLAINED (Englewood Cliffs, NJ: Prentice-Hall, 1972), 39-54; George Eberhart, MONSTERS: A GUIDE TO INFORMATION ON UNACCOUNTED FOR CREATURES, INCLUDING BIGFOOT, MANY WATER MONSTERS, AND OTHER IRREGULAR ANIMALS (NY: Garland, 1983), 81-93; and "Prehistoric Survivors," MAN AND BEAST, 31-3.

15. Scott Doggett, "Adventurer Stalks the Elusive Dinosaur," United Press International, 16 August 1988.

16. G.W.B. Huntingford, "Ghosts and Devils in East Africa," MAN 28:77 (May 1928).

17. Roy Mackal, A LIVING DINOSAUR? (Leiden: Brill, 1987), 39.

18. Attilio Gatti, GREAT MOTHER FOREST (New York: Scribner's, 1937), 23.

19. Letter to the editor from George H. France, FATE, May 1964, pp. 107-8.

20. Maria Leach, ed., STANDARD DICTIONARY OF FOLKLORE, MYTHOLOGY AND LEGEND (New York: Funk & Wagnalls, 1949), I, 441-2.

21. Walter William Skeat, MALAY MAGIC (London: Macmillan, 1900), 110.

22. Barber and Riches, DICTIONARY OF FABULOUS BEASTS, 66.

23. Fay-Cooper Cole, "Traditions of the Tinguian," Field Museum of Natural History, Pub. 180, Anthro. Ser., vol. 14; no. 1, Chicago, 1915, p. 16.

24. Gerald Wood, ANIMAL FACTS AND FEATS (NY: Bantam, 1977), 90.

25. Leslie Brown, EAGLES OF THE WORLD (NY: Universe Books, 1976), 49.

26. Yule, BOOK OF SER MARCO POLO, II, 410.

27. Newton, DICTIONARY OF BIRDS, 286; and Ronald M. Lockley, MAN AGAINST NATURE (London: Andre Deutsch, 1970), 29.

28. Johannes C. Andersen, MYTHS AND LEGENDS OF THE POLYNESIANS (London: Harrap, 1928). 126-9.

29. Gordon McLauchlan, ed., NEW ZEALAND (Singapore: APA Productions, 1985). 135.

30. Andersen, MYTHS AND LEGENDS, 129.

31. Ibid., 130-1.

THUNDERBIRDS

32. Ingersoll, BIRDS IN LEGEND, 192-3.

33. Peter Brookesmith, ed., CREATURES FROM ELSEWHERE (London: Orbis, 1982), 28-31.

34. At www.thisisbradford.co.uk/bradford__district/leisure/books/birds.html.

35. Pouchet, THE UNIVERSE, 253, 255.

36. John Michell and Robert J. M. Rickard, LIVING WONDERS (London: Thames and Hudson, 1982), 138, 140-2.

37. Doug Storer, AMAZING BUT TRUE ANIMALS (Greenwich, CT: Fawcett, 1963), 43-45.

38. Roger A. Caras, DANGEROUS TO MAN (Philadelphia: Chilton, 1964),120, 122; Roger A. Caras, DANGEROUS TO MAN (New York: Holt, Rinehart, and Winston, 1975).

39. Gerald Wood, GUINESS BOOK OF ANIMAL FACTS AND FEATS (New York: Sterling, 1982), 73, 76.

40. Steiner Hunnestad, "Proof and Witnesses to the Eaglenapping" AFTEN-POSTEN (Oslo, Norway), 21 January 1976, p.12. Translated by John Bengtson.

41. John Ashton, CURIOUS CREATURES IN ZOOLOGY (New York: Cassell, 1890), 181-2.

42. Barber and Riches, DICTIONARY OF FABULOUS BEASTS, 151.

43. Keel, MOTHMAN PROPHECIES, 32.

44. "Earthweek" by Steve Newman, Chronicle Features, Milwaukee (Wisconsin) JOURNAL, 6 October 1991, p. J2.

45. Barber and Riches, DICTIONARY OF FABULOUS BEASTS, 95.

46. Frank Chapin Bray, THE WORLD OF MYTHS: A DICTIONARY OF MYTHOLOGY (New York: Crowell, 1935), 49; and Carrington, "Fabulous Birds," 266.

47. Edward A. Armstrong, THE FOLKLORE OF BIRDS (Boston: Houghton-Mifflin, 1958), 129.

48. W.A. Clouston, POPULAR TALES AND FICTIONS: THEIR MIGRATIONS AND TRANSFORMATIONS (Edinburgh: William Blackwood, 1887), I: 166n.

49. Uno Holmberg, MYTHOLOGY OF ALL RACES: SIBERIAN MYTHOL-OGY (1916, reprint, New York: Cooper Square, 1964), IV: 439-40.

50. Margaria Fichtner, "He Flies Through the Air with Greatest of Birds," Miami (Florida) HERALD, 26 February 1983, pp. 1D, 2D. See also S. L. Hendrickson et al., "Low Genetic Variability in the Geographically Widespread Condor," THE CONDOR 105:1-12 (February 2003).

51. Philip Henry Gosse, ROMANCE OF NATURAL HISTORY, v.11 2nd ed. (London: 1861), 119-20.

52. Edmond Temple, TRAVELS IN VARIOUS PARTS OF PERU (London: 1830), II: 414-7.

53. Gosse, ROMANCE OF NATURAL HISTORY, 120-1.

54. H.C. Adams, TRAVELLERS' TALES (1882, reprint New York: Boni & Liveright, 1927), 254.

55. Gerald Wood, ANIMAL FACTS AND FEATS (New York: Doubleday, 1972), 141.

56. Yule, BOOK OF SER MARCO POLO, II: 410.

57. Tony Morrison, LAND ABOVE THE CLOUDS (New York: Universe Books, 1972), 123-4.

58. Leach, DICTIONARY OF FOLKLORE, II: 1111-12; Alfred Metraux, "South American Thunderbirds," JOURNAL OF AMERICAN FOLKLORE 57 (1944): 132-5; and Robert Lowie, BUREAU OF AMERICAN ETHNOLOGY, BULLETIN 143 (3):55, 465.

59. Sebastian Robiou LaMarche, "UFOs and Mysterious Deaths of Animals, Part I: The Animal Deaths in Puerto Rico," FLYING SAUCER REVIEW 22(5):15-18 (1976).

60. Magdalena del Amo-Freixedo, "Current Happenings on Puerto Rico," FLYING SAUCER REVIEW 36(4):19 (Winter 1991).

61. Herman Streibel, "The Sculptures of Santa Lucia Cozumahualpa, Guatemala, in the Hamburg Ethnological Museum," SMITHSONIAN INSTITUTION, ANNUAL REPORT FOR 1899 (Washington: GPO, 1901), 560, Fig. 13; and Curt Muser, comp., FACTS AND ARTIFACTS OF ANCIENT MIDDLE AMERICA (New York: Dutton, 1978), 46.

Chapter 14. Wonder Birds

1. Osmond P. Breland, ANIMAL FACTS AND FALLACIES (New York: Harper, 1948), 86-87.

2. Osmond P. Breland, ANIMAL LIFE AND LORE (New York: Harper, 1963), 149-50.

3. John M. Harris and George T. Jefferson, eds., RANCHO LA BREA: TREASURES OF THE TAR PITS (Los Angeles: Natural History Museum of Los Angeles County, 1985), 56.

4. Hildegarde Howard, "The Incredible Teratorn Again," CONDOR 74 (1972): 343.

5. Hildegarde Howard, "The Prehistoric Avifauna of Smith Creek Cave, Nevada, with a Description of a New Gigantic Raptor," BULLETIN, SO. CALIF. ACADEMY OF SCIENCES 51, pt. 2 (1952): 50-54.

6. Theodore Downs, FOSSIL VERTEBRATES OF SOUTHERN CALIFOR-NIA (Berkeley: University of California Press, 1968), 26.

7. John Wakefield, THE STRANGE WORLD OF BIRDS (Philadelphia: MacRae Smith, 1963), 17-18.

8. Pearl, "Monster Bird," 83.

9. Mary Louise Grossman and John H. Hamlet, BIRDS OF PREY OF THE WORLD (New York: Clarkson N. Potter, 1964), 37.

10. NATIONAL OBSERVER (Dow-Jones weekly), 10 March 1969, p.6.

11. Howard, "Incredible Teratorn Again," 341-4.

12. RES BUREAU BULLETIN (Kingston, Ontario), 23 September 1976 (No.6) and 4 November 1976 (No.8).

13. Associated Press, 16 September 1980; United Press International, 17 September 1980; William R. Long, "Too Big to Fly, Big Bird Ruled Argentine Sky," Miami (Florida) HERALD, 9 October 1981, 1A, 19A, and Kenneth E. Campbell Jr. and Eduardo P. Tonni, "Size and Locomotion in Teratorns (Aves: Teratornithidae)," AUK 100: 390-403 (April 1983).

14. Weight of 265 pounds (120 kilograms) appears in David Boehm, GUIN-NESS 1984 BOOK OF WORLD RECORDS (New York: Sterling, 1983), 80.

15. At www.co.san-bernardino.ca.us/museum/divisions/geo/giant.htm

16. Coleman, CURIOUS ENCOUNTERS, 31-46.

17. Roger L. DiSilvestro, "Saga of AC-9, the Last Free Condor," AUDUBON 89 (July 1987): 12, 14.

18. Sandra Blakeslee, "Straighten up and fly right," NEW YORK TIMES, 3 June 2003.

19. Carl B. Koford, THE CALIFORNIA CONDOR (New York: National Audubon Society, 1953), 8-11, 12.

20. John C. Greenway Jr., EXTINCT AND VANISHING BIRDS OF THE WORLD, rev. ed. (New York: Dover, 1967), 180.

21. Arthur C. Bent, LIFE HISTORIES OF NORTH AMERICAN BIRDS OF PREY, pt. 1 (1937; reprint, New York: Dover, 1961) 2, 12.

22. Schaeffer, "Was the condor known," 181-91.

23. Koford, CALIFORNIA CONDOR, 7.

24. New York TIMES, 12 March 1987, p.B5.

25. "Fossils Extend Condor's Range, Pose Questions," AUDUBON 89 (July 1987): 14.

26. Koford, CALIFORNIA CONDOR, 12.

27. "California Condor in Mexico?" ORYX 16 (May 1981): 21.

28. Kate Callen, "Stalking the Wild California Condor," United Press International, 19 May 1987.

29. James Fisher and Roger Tory Peterson, WORLD OF BIRDS rev. ed. (NY: Crescent, 1977). 36-37.

Chapter 15. Bighoot

1. Michael Fogden, "Fishing Owls, Eagle Owls, and the Snowy Owl," in John A. Burton, ed., OWLS OF THE WORLD: THEIR EVOLUTION, STRUCTURE AND ECOLOGY (New York: Dutton, 1973), 78.

2. At mikeduggan.tripod.com/species/prehistoric.html.

3. JOURNAL OF AMERICAN FOLKLORE 2:230.

4. Richard Carylon, A GUIDE TO THE GODS (NY: Quill, 1982), 35.

5. Erminnie A. Smith, "Myths of the Iroquois," BUREAU OF AMERICAN ETHNOLOGY, SECOND REPORT (1880-81), 59.

6. William Connelly, WYANDOT FOLKLORE (Topeka: Crane, 1899), 85-86.

7. Kathryn Weinstein, OWLS, OWLS, FANTASTIC FOWLS (NY: Arco, 1985), 66.

8. James Owen Dorsey, "Siouan Folklore and Mythologic Notes," AMERI-
   CAN ANTIQUARIAN 7:107 (1885).

9. Clark B. Firestone, THE COASTS OF ILLUSION (NY: Harper, 1924), 74.

10. Lexicographical Centre for Canadian English, A DICTIONARY OF
    CANADIANISMS ON HISTORICAL PRINCIPLES (Toronto: Gage,
    1967), 339.

11. Randolph, WE ALWAYS LIE, 66.

12. James Gay Jones, HAUNTED VALLEY AND MORE FOLK TALES OF
    APPALACHIA (Parsons, WV: McClain Printing, 1979), 31.

13. Helen M. White, "Do Birds Come This Big?" FATE, August 1967, 74-7.

14. John A. Keel, "Mothman Monster," SAGA, October 1968, pp. 34-37, 66-
    70; and John A. Keel, "West Virginia's Enigmatic Bird," FLYING
    SAUCER REVIEW (London), July-August 1968, pp. 7-14.

15. John A. Keel, STRANGE CREATURES FROM TIME AND SPACE
    (Greenwich, Connecticut: Fawcett, 1970), chapter 18; and John A. Keel,
    THE MOTHMAN PROPHECIES (New York: Signet, 1975).

16. White, "Do Birds."

17. Bob Withers, "Two tri-staters add their theories to the mix," Huntington
    (WV) HERALD-DISPATCH, 25 January 2002.

18. Lewis Wayne Walker, "Who's Whoo on the Night Shift," AUDUBON
    MAGAZINE, 51(3): 159 (May-June 1949).

19. BIGFOOT CO-OP (Whittier, CA), Vol. 9, October 1988.

20. Hartley Burr Alexander, MYTHOLOGY OF ALL RACES, Vol. XI (1916),
    329.

21. Mark A. Hall, "Why Nothing Gets Solved in One Lifetime," WONDERS
    8(2):54-63 (June 2003).

Chapter 16. The Challenges of Giant Birds of Prey

1. George M. Eberhart, MYSTERIOUS CREATURES (Santa Barbara: ABC-
   Clio, 2002).

INDEX

PARAVIEW publishes quality works that focus on body, mind, and spirit and the frontiers of science and culture. Our cryptozoology titles include:

Bigfoot! The True Story of Apes in America
Loren Coleman • $14.00/£8.99
Coleman investigates America's biggest mystery—could an unrecognized "ape" be living in our midst? He draws on more than 40 years of investigations, interviews, and fieldwork to reach some surprising conclusions about these animals—our nearest cousins!

Three Men Seeking Monsters: Six Weeks in Pursuit of Werewolves, Lake Monsters, Giant Cats, Ghostly Devil Dogs, and Ape-Men
Nick Redfern • $14.00/£8.99
They sought out the strange. They investigated the inexplicable. They had one hell of a hangover. *Three Men Seeking Monsters* is a uniquely gonzo trek with a trio of adventurers who pushed themselves to the edge—and went right over it.

The Beasts that Hide from Man: Seeking the World's Last Undiscovered Animals
Karl P.N. Shuker, Ph.D. • $17.95/£11.99
Shuker provides entertaining, solidly researched tales about extraordinary animals and also includes a supplement to Bernard Heuvelmans's checklist of cryptozoological animals, which contains updated information on unknown creatures.

The Great New England Sea Serpent: An Account of Unknown Creatures Sighted by Many Respectable Persons Between 1638 and the Present Day
J.P. O'Neill • $15.95/£10.99
O'Neill draws on the historical record as well as previously unpublished first-hand accounts to chronicle more than 230 sightings of mysterious marine creatures inhabiting the Gulf of Maine. This book is for all the people who look at the sea, and wonder…

Mysterious America: The Revised Edition
Loren Coleman • $16.95/£12.99
Coleman has thoroughly updated his highly praised 1983 classic. "Simply put, this is the best book I have ever read on the subject of America's mysteries."
—Derek Anderson, *Stranger Things*.

Mothman and Other Curious Encounters
Loren Coleman • $14.95/£11.99
On November 15, 1966, the appearance of "Mothman," a winged, red-eyed creature, set off 13 months of otherworldly mystery, madness, and mayhem. Coleman looks at its precursors, then brings the story up to date with recent sightings of its spawn.

In The Big Thicket: On the Trail of the Wild Man
Rob Riggs • $13.95/£10.99
In the Big Thicket, ghost lights, phantom Indians, howling ape-like "wild men," and fireballs that streak through the nighttime skies defy both our commonsense notions of space and time and all attempts at scientific explanation.

P A R A V I E W

PARAVIEW

publishes quality works that focus on body, mind,
and spirit; the frontiers of science and culture;
and responsible business—areas related to
the transformation of society.

PARAVIEW PUBLISHING

offers books via three imprints.

PARAVIEW POCKET BOOKS
are traditionally published books co-published by
Paraview and Simon & Schuster's Pocket Books.

PARAVIEW PRESS and *PARAVIEW SPECIAL EDITIONS*
use digital print-on-demand technology to create
original paperbacks for niche audiences,
as well as reprints of previously
out-of-print titles.

For a complete list of **PARAVIEW** Publishing's books
and ordering information, please visit our website at
www.paraview.com, where you can also sign up
for our free monthly media guide.

TRANSFORMING THE WORLD
ONE BOOK AT A TIME

Printed in the United States
35638LVS00006B/58-66